Seth Lindstromberg
Frank Boers

Teaching Chunks of Language
From noticing to remembering

HELBLING
LANGUAGES

Teaching Chunks of Language
by Seth Lindstromberg and Frank Boers

© HELBLING LANGUAGES 2008
www.helblinglanguages.com

First published 2008
ISBN 978-3-85272-056-2

Edited by Jane Arnold and Mari Carmen Fonseca
Copy edited by Caroline Petherick
Designed by Quantico
Cover design by Capolinea
Illustrations by Piet Lüthi

The illustrations on p.134 are by Tessa Woodward
Photo on p.130 by kind permission of the Tall Ships Youth Trust

Printed by Bieffe

Contents

CHAPTER 1
HOW TO USE THIS BOOK

Chapter 1: How to use this book

At the core of the Lexical Approach to learning English is the belief that ambitious students need to acquire masses of multi-word 'chunks of language'.[G] But the techniques and exercises characteristic of this approach do not furnish teachers with an adequate means of helping students remember those hundreds or thousands of additional, complex, items of vocabulary. Consequently, within the Lexical Approach so far, the student has been like someone expected to row across an ocean in a very leaky boat, and the teacher, frustratingly, has been given no adequate way of helping them. We hope this book will begin to change things for the better.

1.1 What are 'chunks of language'?

What we call a 'chunk of language' is a sequence of words which native speakers feel is the natural and preferred way of expressing a particular idea or purpose. Frequently, there are various combinations of different words that can convey a certain message. Typically, though, only one or two of these combinations have become accepted as normal and natural. Thus, all three of the following can be understood by a native English speaker: *Time will show, The future will reveal, The future will tell* ... but the phrase which has become the standard expression of the underlying idea is *Time will tell.* That is to say, *Time will tell* is a 'chunk', whereas the other three phrases are not; and if you did use any of them, your English at that point would be odd.

1.2 Who is this book for? What gap does it fill?

We have written this book for EFL/ESL teachers working with teenagers and young adults who would like to become fluent and expressive in English. One group within this readership is teachers whose students might go on to take one of the higher level international exams such as the Cambridge First Certificate in English, Certificate in Advanced English or Certificate of Proficiency in English.

Although a number of the exercises and activity sequences in this book can be used effectively in beginner and elementary classes, our main focus is on learners in the pre-intermediate to advanced range. There are two reasons for this focus. Firstly,

with respect to chunks of language, teachers at beginner and elementary levels seem relatively well aided by existing course materials, in comparison with teachers of higher level learners. Secondly, the chunks that are appropriate for beginner and elementary classes tend to occur in authentic speech and writing so often that learners may well be able to pick them up on their own.

In considering the needs of learners who wish to become good users of English, we found that one weakness of existing course books in the pre-intermediate–advanced range is that they do not target enough chunks. More seriously, the methods employed in these books do not do enough to help learners remember the chunks they meet. Because many students want to learn more chunks than are targeted in their course books, publishers have come out with an impressive number of supplementary books – ones focusing on idioms and phrasal verbs are especially numerous. However, the methods which these books employ are similar to those of existing course books, except that they tend to be particularly limited in the types of exercises they include. And it has become clear over time that those methods are inefficient, with the result that students' learning is relatively slow and unproductive, which is, in turn, frustrating for the teacher.

This is the background against which we decided to write the book you are now looking at. We hope it will be a useful addition to your repertoire of teaching resources, providing an extra way of encouraging students' learning, and increasing both their and your enjoyment.

1.3 How is it organised?

This introduction sets out the rationale for the methods and techniques you will find in the remaining chapters of the book:

- Chapter 2 describes basic procedures for helping learners to notice chunks and to *begin* to remember them.
- In Chapter 3, we describe ways of teaching that make chunks especially memorable. Because teachers must do much more than just teach chunks, this chapter also provides students with opportunities to learn

single word vocabulary and to speak, listen, read, and write chunks.

- Chapter 4 illustrates techniques of reviewing and quizzing which you can apply to chunks of various kinds.
- And these are followed by the photocopiable material linked to the activities in the three main chapters, and the Keys to the exercises.

1.4 What kinds of chunks are there?

Chunks are diverse in type. One way of classifying them is by function, e.g. conversational fillers such as *sort of,* and *you know what I mean;* exclamations, *Good God!, Trick or treat!;* pragmatic notices, *Excuse me, How are you doing?;* discourse organisers, *Having said that, The thing is;* and situation evaluators, *Small world!, It's a Catch-22 situation.*

Or they may be classified more on the basis of form, e.g. sentence heads such as *Could you … ?, Why not … ?;* phrasal verbs, *break down, wipe out;* compounds: *credit card, weather forecast;* strong collocations, *tell a story, stark naked;* and grammatical frames, *as … as …,* and *the -er the -er.*

They may also be laid out on a continuum extending from chunks whose meaning is immediately clear *(please come in!)* to ones whose meaning seems impossible to guess *(hit it off with someone).*

Or they may be categorised by geographical variety (e.g. international, British or the south east of England), by the age of typical users (e.g. people over 60, teens), by level of formality (formal, informal, slang), and so on.

One family of chunks which has received a lot of attention in TESOL includes chunks that seem to be more or less idiomatic, figurative idioms like *make ends meet,* similes like *blind as a bat,* and proverbs like *The early bird catches the worm.*

But there are other families of chunks too, such as ones that are common in everyday language *(never mind, as soon as possible);* ones that are not *(be that as it may);* ones typical of specific domains of life *(hold someone in custody)* or typical of a particular genre *(conduct an experiment).* Some chunks go out of fashion *(raining cats and dogs).* But every year newly coined word sequences, such as *broadband,* come to be used as chunks.

Native speakers acquire most of their repertoire of lexical chunks through multiple encounters with particular word combinations, or 'word strings'[G], from early childhood on. As the amount and kind of language that is heard and read throughout life varies from individual to individual, a degree of idiosyncrasy in the mental chunk repertoires of individual speakers is to be expected. For example, *unbroken night's sleep* may be a chunk that is familiar to parents, nannies and nurses, but not to some other people. Still, we may assume that there is a core of lexical chunks that is common to the repertoires of most native speakers of English. For example, when we asked five native speaker teachers of English to indicate in the text on the next page the word strings they felt to be chunks, their choices showed considerable divergence – but they did unanimously agree on the 'chunk status' of the strings we have underlined.

As you can see, even these relatively few chunks vary in terms of form and function. They also vary in commonness, or frequency. A chunk we might encounter or use several times a day is for example, but some of the others (e.g. *preach to the converted, set the tone for, in the face of*) we would encounter or use only very occasionally. Nevertheless, the overwhelming majority of native speakers would instantly and unanimously recognise even those last three word strings as chunks.

1.5 Why is knowing lots of chunks so useful?

By definition, a chunk is a string of words that we can find in our memory as a ready-made unit. Knowing lots of chunks contributes to fluent speaking and writing because we can just pluck them out of our memories whole, without having to mentally construct them word by word.

Every time we can use a chunk of words as a single unit, we free up thinking capacity that we can then devote to planning and delivering an upcoming stretch of talk or writing that does not consist of chunks and which we cannot avoid putting together word by word. Knowing lots of chunks also makes listening and reading easier. This is because each time we recognise a chunk and understand it as a single unit, we gain

Schools encouraged to <u>get in touch</u> with pupils' emotions

Last week the American psychologist Daniel Goleman told a full assembly of British headmasters and teachers that <u>test results</u> and learning will improve in schools if the principles of <u>emotional intelligence</u> are adopted. In his speech Dr Goleman emphasised that emotional intelligence <u>is not about</u> becoming more emotional. Instead, it means being intelligent about your emotions and managing them well, knowing your own emotional state and how it is affecting your decisions. It is about being skilled in relationships.

He was <u>preaching to the converted</u> – many colleges <u>are</u> already <u>keen on</u> promoting emotional intelligence. Most teachers <u>are receptive to</u> Goleman's ideas because they instinctively understand that children learn better when they are not tense or upset. <u>In the same way</u> teachers nurture children's work in the classroom, a headmaster can <u>set the tone for</u> the school and <u>get the best out</u> of staff.

In some British schools the concept of EQ (emotional intelligence) is being implemented by letting the pupils score themselves and each other against different emotional skills and then using the results to <u>set personal targets</u> for themselves. <u>For example</u>, when pupils have identified they <u>have a tendency to</u> just <u>give up</u> when <u>confronted with problems</u>, they are encouraged to <u>set the target</u> for themselves to keep persisting <u>in the face of setbacks</u>. Other activities include the use of "feelings charts". The children have personal charts to show how they are feeling each day. This way the teacher can gauge the mood in the room and adjust their approach accordingly. It also helps identify troubled children who may <u>need special attention</u>. Using dance to combat <u>low self esteem</u> is another technique being explored. Schools have found that <u>by the age of</u> 10 or 11 boys usually do not want to be involved in dance because they think it's embarrassing. So the schools got them doing the Haka – the dance performed by the New Zealand rugby team – and that <u>made a real difference</u>. In another school, children are invited to <u>give each other compliments</u> <u>at the end of</u> a class. <u>The traditional view is that</u> it's not a teacher's job <u>to get involved with</u> how kids feel about themselves. But a lot of kids don't learn because they're not in a state where they are ready to learn.

The notion of emotional intelligence – the ability to understand and control your emotions, and recognise and respond to those of others – was first popularised in the mid-nineties. Today it is emerging as <u>the single most important</u> and effective business and personal skill of the new century. It is claimed to be <u>twice as important as</u> cognitive or technical skills for <u>high job performance</u> and it is said to be virtually all-important at top level. Analysing the profiles of <u>top executives</u> in 15 global companies, including IBM, PepsiCo and Volvo, Dr. Goleman found that what distinguished the 'star' performers was not superior technical or intellectual ability but emotional competence: <u>political awareness</u>, self-confidence, drive and influence. While IQ <u>has traditionally been</u> <u>the means by which</u> we judge someone's abilities and potential, EQ is the new benchmark for a <u>new world</u>. <u>If you've got it</u>, you're <u>more likely to be</u> powerful, successful and have fulfilling relationships than if you haven't.

From *The Guardian*, 14 April 2003

a little time which we can then devote to the in-between stretches of talk or print which are worded less conventionally. When language learners begin to mentally process word strings like native speakers do (i.e. as chunks), they reap these same benefits.

In addition, using chunks makes learners seem more proficient and idiomatic. Moreover, if the chunks that a learner knows are *well embedded* in long–term memory, these chunks may serve the learner as 'islands of accuracy' that reduce the overall risk of making mistakes or of producing odd word combinations. Even very proficient second- or foreign-language learners may attract unwelcome attention by using phrasing which is grammatical but odd. Often, this is because of mother tongue influence. For example, French learners may produce the unnatural expression *realise a survey* (instead of *conduct a survey*) because *realise a survey* closely resembles a chunk that exists in French. But learners may also produce an unnatural word combination simply because they have never encountered or never managed to remember the natural alternative. Teaching chunks can help students use natural phrasing more often.

1.6 How great is the challenge of learning chunks?

According to some estimates, about half of everyday English discourse is made up of strings of frequently co-occurring words. Consider idioms, which make up just one type of chunk: idiom dictionaries for learners of English typically contain no fewer than 4,000 entries. If you take other types of chunks into consideration as well, it soon becomes clear that the size of the English repertoire of chunks in general must be enormous. For example, the *Oxford Collocations Dictionary for Students of English* (2002) mentions no fewer than 150,000 collocations, and even this is far from an exhaustive inventory.

Given the enormous size of the English repertoire of chunks, one might wonder how students can ever get to grips with it, especially in contexts of classroom–based instruction where their exposure to the target language is a minuscule fraction of the years and years which enable native speakers to learn these chunks so well.

Fortunately, many of the chunks in English belong to specific domains (e.g. economics) and specific genres (e.g. academic writing) and are therefore not of immediate concern to learners of English in general. Furthermore, many additional chunks are used so infrequently that we can discount them, too, as primary targets for teaching/learning; and still other chunks may be discounted because they belong to a variety of English that we give a lower priority to. But even with these subtractions, students wanting to attain good proficiency face the daunting challenge of mastering *a great many chunks.* On top of this, there is the extra challenge of not simply learning chunks well enough to recognise them, but of learning them so well that they can quickly be remembered and used in production as and when needed.

1.7 How do chunks invite targeted teaching in class?

You may wonder why learners can't just accumulate good knowledge of chunks incidentally from the discourse they experience, e.g. in reading, like native speakers do. However, we now know that in the case of learners this kind of 'incidental' acquisition of words and chunks proceeds very slowly. Here are some of the reasons why:

1) A new word or chunk must be met multiple times *within a relatively short time span* before it leaves any stable trace in memory. But two key facts must be noted:

   a) Only high frequency words or chunks are likely to occur regularly enough for this process of incidental uptake to be successful.

   b) But the vast majority of words and chunks are not highly frequent.

Take another look at the chunks underlined in the article from *The Guardian* in Section 1.5; few of those chunks, if any, are likely to be encountered in normal authentic discourse often enough within a sufficiently short span of time for them to become well embedded, or 'entrenched', in a learner's memory through incidental uptake.

2) In everyday communication, we tend not to pay simultaneous attention to both meaning and linguistic form. Rather, we tend to focus on the meaning of messages, and as long as communication proceeds smoothly we direct little attention to exact wording, word endings and so on. For example, when we listen to the radio news, it is usually the news itself that we are interested in rather than the exact words used by the news reader. And when we read a novel or a short story, we are normally interested in the storyline; rarely will we notice the exact wording well enough to be able to remember it even in the short term. Language learners tend to be no different. In fact, it is well established that learners are unlikely to pay much attention to unfamiliar words while they are processing discourse for content/meaning. They are even less likely to devote attention to more complex *patterns of co-occurrence* of words.

For example, if both of the keywords that make up a strong collocation (e.g. make an effort) are familiar, and if the meaning of the collocation is perfectly clear, few learners are likely to devote to the collocation anything like the attention needed to store it in memory as a chunk. This is why learners persist in transferring collocational patterns from their mother tongue to the target language with such unnatural results as *do an effort, *do a mistake, *make an experience and *depend from. When one of the words in a chunk does happen to be unfamiliar – as the word tether might be in the chunk at the end of (my) tether, learners will sometimes try to guess its meaning or take the time to look it up, at least if they believe understanding the word is crucial for text comprehension. But what they are still unlikely to do, without prompting from a teacher, is to examine the words around tether and then decide to remember the phrase as a whole.

Actually, a learner is most likely to pay attention to a chunk when *all* the words are unfamiliar, as might be the case for wreak havoc. It could then be that the words might leave a trace in a learner's memory in association with each other. However, this illustrates another hindrance to the incidental learning of chunks. On average, a long word is harder to remember than a short word. A chunk is likely to be longer than the average single word. Therefore, learning a chunk that consists completely of unfamiliar words (e.g. wreak havoc) is bound to be relatively difficult to learn, simply because it is, as a whole, likely to be relatively long.

3) Contexts which are informative enough to enable learners to guess the meanings of unfamiliar words are fairly rare. And it is well known that not only do few learners make regular use of dictionaries but also that learners are prone to using their dictionaries ineffectively. Thus, even when learners do notice and pay attention to an unfamiliar item of vocabulary – be it a word or a phrase – there is no guarantee at all that they will correctly identify its meaning, especially if they don't meet it very often. Plus, when learners do look up the meaning of a word in a dictionary, the chances are low that they will find, notice and remember useful information about how that word combines with other words. It is true that specialised learners' dictionaries of idioms, phrasal verbs and collocations are increasingly available, at least for English – but it does not appear that the average learner makes use of one. For one thing, there is the serious inconvenience of needing to use a general dictionary for ordinary word lookups, an idiom dictionary for idiom lookups, and then a phrasal verb dictionary for phrasal verb lookups, and so on. (The Oxford Collocations Dictionary, for instance, gives no information about meanings.) Fortunately, publishers are producing general learners' dictionaries with more and more information about chunking; The Macmillan English Dictionary for Advanced Learners (2nd ed., 2007) is particularly good in this regard.

In sum, we cannot take it for granted that our students will somehow manage to pick up lots of chunks in the course of their use of normal meaning-focused language, not even if the English they hear and read is extensive, authentic and largely comprehensible to them.

Consequently, if we want our students to learn and remember useful numbers of chunks, we need to do something in class to help them. As other authors have said, raising students' awareness of the importance of chunks is a useful first step. But we also need to introduce activities for speeding up the acquisition of particular chunks, and that means that we should treat the chunks we target in ways which encourage their long term entrenchment [G] in memory. The main purpose of this book is to demonstrate ways of doing this.

1.8 How can we make the best use of scarce class time?

Our three–stage programme for chunk learning is reflected in the organisation of this book:
1 to help students notice chunks and appreciate their importance (Chapter 2);
2 to deliberately target selected sets of chunks and apply techniques known to help students commit chunks to memory (Chapter 3); and
3 to consolidate knowledge through review (Chapter 4).

Given all the thousands of lexical chunks that exist, we must be selective about the ones we focus on in the limited class time available. The criterion for selection that is most commonly mentioned is that of frequency of occurrence; in a nutshell, high frequency chunks should get priority.

One way of getting a rough idea of the relative frequency of a chunk – a way that is open to anybody with internet access – is simply through doing a Google 'exact word' search. In this way, we can confirm that of course and *by the way* are extremely frequent in English, with 259 and 69.4 million hits, respectively (as on 21 April 2008). *In the wake of,* with 2,990,000 hits, was markedly less common, but can still be called frequent. *Plain sailing*, with 230,000 hits, is in the middle range of frequency for a chunk; **and** *hobbled by debt*, which came up only 397 times, is one we can classify as pretty rare.

As it happens, the inconvenient truth about chunks is that the vast majority of them are not highly frequent at all; instead, they are either in the middle or the rare range. And those relatively few chunks which are highly frequent – e.g. conversational fillers such as *kind of* and *you know what I mean* – are precisely the ones we probably don't need to spend class time on anyway because learners really do have a good chance of just picking them up by hearing and reading them again and again. So, although when selecting chunks to focus on in this book we have taken the criterion of frequency into account, we have also included a number of chunks that belong to middle frequency range – ones like *plain sailing,* for instance.

Because ambitious learners must go far beyond the relatively few chunks that are highly frequent, the other selection criterion that we have adopted is one that is not often mentioned in the literature on vocabulary teaching – the presence of the **linguistic motivation** G of a chunk. Since linguistic motivation significantly increases the ease with which a chunk can be remembered, this second criterion could be called the criterion of **memorability**.

1.9 How can chunks be 'motivated'?

When we say in this book that particular chunks are (linguistically) motivated, we mean that their wording is partly explainable in terms of identifiable influences. Let's look at three particularly important kinds of motivation of chunks:

The influence of the past, of culture, and of economics: the meaning of many idioms is explainable in terms of their original literal meaning and usage. For example, the idiomatic meaning of *show someone the ropes* (= teach someone how to perform a task) makes perfect sense – i.e. is not arbitrary – if you know that originally this expression was used to refer to occasions on which an experienced sailor would show a novice seaman how to handle the ropes on a sailing ship. Thus,

the existence in English of the chunk *show someone the ropes* is partly explained by the fact that for centuries seafaring was an important part of British life, with great social, cultural and economic significance.

The influence of register and genre: in the expression *remain* in custody, the use of the relatively formal, Latin-derived remain instead of the less formal, Germanic verb stay becomes understandable when we recall that English discourse which has to do with very formal settings tends itself to be consistently formal – i.e. derived from Norman French or Latin – in wording. So for the formal, Latinate, legal word *custody* the word *remain* is a better companion than *stay.*

The influence of repetition of sounds: in the chunk *it takes two to tango* the choice of *tango* rather than, say, *waltz* or *jive* is almost certainly motivated by the appeal of the alliteration – the repetition of the 't' sound at the beginnings of the words.

Chunks that are motivated lend themselves well to instruction that stimulates *insightful learning,* as opposed to blind memorisation. Insightful learning is well known to promote long term retention of vocabulary in the memory. In other words, we are not claiming that *all* chunks can be taught in terms of linguistic motivation; still, as we hope to demonstrate, the different kinds of linguistic motivation do, collectively, cover a fair proportion of all the chunks that an ambitious learner might wish to be able to understand, remember and use.

1.10 How can we help our students remember chunks? What about using mnemonics? G

One remedy that is sometimes proposed for the difficulty of remembering new vocabulary is the use of specialised techniques called 'mnemonics'. But unfortunately these have all been designed to enable the recall of single words, and few mnemonics, if any, are easy to apply to chunks.

Take, for example, the well known 'keyword method', where a word in the students' mother tongue (L_1) is used as a ' key', or prompt, in order to enable the recall of a word in the target language (L_2). This works by choosing an L_1 word which not only bears a formal resemblance to the L_2 word but which also has a meaning that can be associated with it. For instance, the Dutch word *bleek* ('pale') may serve as a keyword for the retrieval of the

English target word *bleach;* and the Dutch *puntje* ('the sharp end of a pointed object') may serve as a keyword for recollecting the English word *puncture.* But applying this technique to chunks takes a good deal of creative thinking. For one thing, it is almost always difficult to think of an L1 prompt for a *whole* L_2 chunk. At best, a learner is likely to be able to think of a prompt for just one word in a target chunk – and this is bound to reduce the effectiveness of the mnemonic. Suppose, for example, a Dutch learner wants to memorise the English chunk *the more the merrier.* A possible Dutch keyword could be *merrie* (= mare) because it formally resembles *merrier* and because the learner could imagine mares happily running about in a meadow because they like each other's company. But, as previously mentioned, this keyword prompts only part of the form of the chunk; it certainly does not prompt the construction *the … the …,* and probably not *more* either.

A further problem with using the keyword method to try to remember a chunk is that learners need prompts that also remind them of the overall meaning of the chunk. And integrating this extra dimension into a keyword prompt tends to be extremely tricky.

Must chunks always be treated as wholes?

Given the difficulty of using mnemonics in the teaching and learning of chunks, it is fortunate that other means of helping students remember chunks are available, ones which exploit the types of linguistic motivation mentioned in Section 1.9. For example, many proverbs (which tend to be relatively long as chunks go and which therefore ought to be especially hard to remember) rhyme, e.g. *When the cat's away, the mice will play.* Many other proverbs show alliteration, like *He who pays the piper calls the tune,* or assonance, like *The squeaky wheel gets the grease.* Many idioms and common sayings show either these same three patterns (sometimes in combination) or repetition of entire words, e.g. *Boys will be boys, neck and neck.* Another common pattern which can help a learner remember a chunk is seen in *aches and pains,* where each word can remind the learner of the other (i.e. aches can remind a learner of the word pains and vice versa). There is solid evidence that all such patterns make chunks relatively easy to remember. But we teachers cannot assume that learners will notice these patterns by themselves, so it is often going to be up to us to bring them to our students' attention.

What can we help our students notice and reflect on?

The usefulness of chunks comes most to the fore when they are so well entrenched in memory that we can automatically use and recognise them as units even when we are in the midst of communication and are concentrating on other things. The fact that this is the desired end result of chunk learning does not mean that we should discourage learners from devoting attention to the word-by-word make-up of L_2 chunks. Far from it – noticing and examining chunks on a word-by-word basis can be extremely fruitful stages in the learning process.

First, let's consider the matter of the word-by-word meaning of a chunk. It may well be true that good users of English are unaware of the literal sense of the word *square* every time they use or encounter the chunk *back to square one.* But if you are trying to help students remember this phrase, it can be helpful to them to point out that in this chunk the word *square* relates to a position on a game board rather than to, say, a square in town (= a small park or plaza). Put generally, simply informing learners about the literal sense or origin of one or more of its key words can facilitate overall comprehension, enhance retention in memory, and even help learners appreciate connotations and usage restrictions.[G]

Something similar applies to sound and spelling. Many users of English are unlikely to be aware of the alliteration in *Time will tell* whenever they use this expression. But alliteration – provided the learners become aware of it – can make a chunk easier for them to remember.

Importantly, it is known that learners on their own are unlikely either to correctly guess the original sense of key words in many idioms or to notice sound patterns such as alliteration. Consequently, there is a need for a good deal of teacher-led guidance. The payoff can be significantly higher rates of remembering.

In the light of all this, let's now look in some more detail at the kinds of information processing that are promoted by the activities described in Chapter 3. The main broad aim is to encourage students to engage in the kind of relatively rich, deep, 'elaborative'[G] mental processing which is known to enhance retention of vocabulary in memory. In practice, this means teachers helping students to learn target chunks insightfully;

and this means exploiting the non-arbitrary, motivated properties of chunks of language.

What are the benefits of noticing and appreciating the imagery of figurative expressions?

The figures of speech that we hear about most often are:

Simile (explicit comparison): *I can hear you as clear as a bell*.

Metaphor (implicit, deeply suggestive, often image-rich comparison): *life is a journey*, which gives us the idea that a life can include crossroads, sidetracks, obstacles, partings of ways, and so on, or *my patience snapped*, which depicts patience as being something brittle, like a stick.

Metonymy (where one thing stands for another, provided that in daily life the two things are often found in association): *Could you give me a hand?*, in which *hand* stands for 'help' because a typical and conspicuous way of helping people involves using a hand.

Many target chunks can be grouped according to overarching metaphorical themes (e.g. from the theme of life being a journey we derive *being at a crossroads in life, reaching a turning point,* etc), or according to the domains of life in which these chunks were originally used (e.g. from sewing: *I've lost my thread, I'm at a loose end* etc).

When students successfully group such chunks by theme or domain of activity, they engage in 'resuscitation of literal senses'. This is mnemonically helpful in at least four respects.

1 **Grouping:** this lends a sense of organisation to the encounter with the vocabulary in question; and organised input is known to be easier to learn than input which is jumbled.

2 **Matching chunks with domains of activity:** this is likely to evoke mental images of concrete scenes. Each such image is capable of becoming part of the learner's understanding of the word. This happens when new neural pathways form to link memory traces for the target chunk (e.g. the memory traces of its wording) to the memory traces of a particular image. This linkage apparently begins when both the target chunk and the image are being held in a learner's working memory *at the same time*. The more extensive the learner's existing network of traces and pathways in their brain, the easier it is for them to locate a chunk in memory.

3 **Linking a chunk with rich mental images:** this facilitates appreciation of any restrictions on its usage. For example, it is commonly observed that students may learn an expression, but not learn it well enough to use it in a natural way; thus a student may say, *"In the wake of dinner, we watched TV,"* which violates the usage restriction that *in the wake of* is generally followed by a term for a major event such as a hurricane or a crucial election. However, knowledge of the relevant literal meaning of *wake* (a trail of disturbed water behind something relatively large like a moving ship) is knowledge that can help a student remember that *in the wake of* does not simply mean 'later in time'.

The kind of image-rich knowledge of literal meanings that we are speaking of can also help learners cope with puns, which often hinge on the figurative (as against literal) ambiguity of words and idioms.

4 **Exploration of chunks in relation to particular domains of activity:** this may foster a certain degree of cultural awareness because domains of life that are prominent in a given community are likely to leave a clear stamp on that community's repertoire of idioms. For example, idioms from the language of horse riding and racing are likely to be particularly engaging and effective if used in a context that has a connection with the great importance of horses in Britain and Ireland in the past, and the popularity of recreational horse riding and racing in the present.

What is involved in noticing 'catchy' sound patterning, and what is the benefit?

The English storehouse of chunks abounds in catchy sound patterning. Such catchiness is probably one reason why certain chunks become conventionalised in the first place, which would contribute to explaining why we say: *be left high and dry* (rather than the non-rhyming *be left up and dry),* and *the more the merrier* (rather than the non-alliterative *the more the happier*).

Taken together, the two patterns of sound repetition, **rhyme** and **alliteration**, help explain the choice of words in up to 20% of the chunks included in English idiom dictionaries, with alliteration being especially common. There is also statistical evidence that alliteration plays a part in the formation of compounds, a type of chunk which is very important in English, e.g. *baby boom, bargain basement, body blow, backbone.*

The fact that so many chunks display these mnemonic patterns is good news. Even better news is the fact that other, less noticeable, kinds of sound repetition can also facilitate remembering, i.e. vowel repetition, or **assonance**, as in *small talk*. In addition, consonant repetition generally, or **consonance**, e.g. *a casual acquaintance,* almost certainly makes chunks relatively memorable.

As you will see in Chapters 3 and 4, awareness of such patterns of sound repetition can be fostered in a number of ways, e.g. by giving students mixed lists of known chunks to sort according to the type of sound pattern they exhibit. Chunks to which they pay special attention are particularly likely to be remembered later on.

What is 'semantic prosody', and how can awareness of it help learners?

Semantic prosody is the term for how words with similar register and connotation are often found in each other's company. To give two examples:

1. The rather legalistic, Latinate verb *commit* collocates with legalistic, mostly Latinate nouns such as *crime, offence, murder, adultery, suicide* – all words to do with breaking laws (both adultery and suicide used to be considered crimes in Britain). None of these nouns is a natural partner for the non-legalistic, non-Latinate verb *do.*
2. The formal verb *seek* tends to collocate with nouns such as *solace* and *solitude* – nouns that are like it in being rather formal.

If students are made aware of this non-arbitrary dimension of word partnerships, they may, when in doubt about the right choice between two synonyms needed to complete
a chunk, begin to make better educated guesses.

What about cases of multiple motivation?

Many figurative chunks that become easier for learners to remember when they explore their underlying imagery also show catchy sound patterns – e.g. *dish the dirt on someone* (= tell scandalous news about someone). To give another example, sound repetition and semantic prosody sometimes combine – e.g. *seek*

+ *solace, solitude, sympathy, asylum.* This allows repeat targeting of the same chunks in quite different activities, and pointing out double or multiple motivation can help learners consolidate their knowledge of targeted chunks. Additionally, adopting different vantage points in working with chunks is likely to cater to the needs of learners with different cognitive styles.

1.11   About the downloadable worksheets

A package of additional worksheets for chunk learning can be downloaded from www.helblinglanguages.com/teachingchunks.
It targets sets of idiomatic expressions that are signalled in the (corpus based) *Collins Cobuild Dictionary of Idioms* (2002) as 'frequently used'. It also lists a considerable number of miscellaneous other chunks (compounds, collocations, similes and more) selected from the (corpus based) *Oxford Collocations Dictionary for Students of English* (2002). These worksheets can be used either in the classroom or at home.

The greater part of the package consists of 'fill-in-the-missing-words' exercises, which are usually provided in different versions of varying levels of difficulty. For example, one version may contain cues (such as the first letter of the missing word being given) that are absent from the later, more challenging, version of the same exercise. Which version of an exercise you choose will obviously depend on the level of your students.

Additionally, a same-level gap fill exercise will typically also be provided in two versions that are identical except that different words are missing from the same chunks (e.g. _____ *will tell and Time will* _____). In other words, Version A can serve as a key for the right answers to Version B, and vice versa. You could thus give half of a group of students Version A of a gap fill exercise and give the other half Version B, and then get them to swap worksheets so they can supplement each other's answers.

1.12   Finally, some recommendations for vocabulary teaching in general

Because chunks can be considered as one specific type of vocabulary, certain general truths about teaching and learning vocabulary are likely to apply also to the teaching and learning of chunks:

1. An excellent way for learners to entrench knowledge of vocabulary in memory is to guess its meaning

from context. But you do need to remember that such guessing is not very likely to be successful, and so learners typically require very careful guidance.

2 Learners should meet new vocabulary in doses that are manageable for them.

3 Putting target items into a narrative makes those items especially easy to remember.

4 It is helpful to students if they can use new vocabulary meaningfully and creatively.

5 Items in batches of new vocabulary should not be too similar to one another in sound or spelling; simultaneous or consecutive presentation of, for example, the phrasal verbs _take_ in (a lodger), _take_ on (a challenge), _take_ to (someone) and _take_ up (a pastime) is fraught with the risk that learners will get confused about which of these phrasal verbs means what.

6 If wholly new items which are very similar in meaning to each other are encountered at the same time, they can be hard to remember. It may be appropriate to teach a lesson on such sets in order to help students see how the individual chunks differ in meaning, but this is best done in higher level classes where students have already achieved a basic understanding of much of the vocabulary in question

7 Review is crucial. So for review, keep a note of items – including chunks – which you deem to be important. To be ready for Activity 3.17 in particular, record, as you come across them, chunks with word repetition, rhyme, consonance, alliteration, alliteration and other consonant repetition, and assonance.

And now, the activities!

CHAPTER 2
BASIC CHUNK TEACHING ACTIVITIES
– INITIAL STEPS TOWARDS MEMORISATION

Introduction

This chapter presents basic activities for helping your students to notice chunks and to become aware of their form and meaning/function. These activities involve a good deal of what memory researchers call 'rehearsal'.[G] This learning practice has a lot in common with what actors do in order to remember their lines through practising them again and again. In its simplest form, rehearsal can simply consist in repeating chunks out loud or copying them onto paper.

More complex and effective forms of rehearsal involve the extra mental effort of holding one or more target chunks in mind for a while (perhaps even for less than a minute) before using them to complete some sort of task. Such effortful remembering and retrieval plays an important part in forming durable memories of targeted chunks, and the tasks in this chapter are well suited to making this happen. You may already be familiar with some, or all, of them. Here, though, they have been adapted in order to focus especially on chunk learning.

For each activity you want to prepare, when you read through the text for the first time you will need to have to hand a photocopy of the relevant sheets from the examples section; this means you will fully understand how that activity works.

Finally, a reminder for when you use these activities: keep a record of the chunks you want to target in later reviewing activities, especially 3.17.

2.1 Reading out loud with pauses

> This exercise can be useful preparation for a number of other exercises in this book because it is designed to make your students more aware of how they can use pausing to be more comprehensible and to hold a listener's attention well. Also, because it involves breaking a text up into shorter sections, it can help your students *notice* and *think about* chunks that are in the text that you use.

Focus   Any kind of chunk; intensive listening & reading; an aspect of pronunciation

Level   Pre-intermediate–Advanced

Time   10–15 minutes

Materials   A set of handouts (or projectable display) (see pp.101-102)

Preparation

1. Choose a short text which includes a number of useful chunks. Brief reports of the day's news are particularly suitable. See also the sample texts.

2. Read the text out aloud to yourself - very dramatically, as if you were a TV news announcer and as if this were *extremely* serious and important news and you wanted to be understood even by listeners with poor hearing or TVs/radios that produce unclear sound. As you read, try to notice natural pause points. Here are some basic guidelines:

   - If you start with a written text, virtually any punctuation mark indicates a pause. Dashes and semi-colons tend to indicate longer pauses than commas. Ends of sentences are natural places to make even longer pauses.

   - Non-defining relative clauses (i.e. descriptions that provide an extra bit of information to the text, but are not essential to its meaning) are set off between a pair of pauses.

   - There are, in general, no pauses inside short prepositional phrases (e.g. *by the way, of course, at work*), between verb and direct object (e.g. *find the time, have fun!*), or inside common chunks generally (e.g. *the day before yesterday, it doesn't matter, get up*).

   - Pauses for dramatic effect can occur where normal pauses might not (e.g. *I hear someone // laughing.*)

   - Speakers have considerable flexibility about where to pause – and in this exercise, the more pauses the better. However, if you have any doubt whether it is possible to pause at a certain point, don't.

3. Lay the text out in a way that highlights the pauses you identify. In the example:

   - a big gap between words on the same line = a minor pause point
   - the end of a line = a conspicuous pause point
   - any comma, dash, bracket, semi-colon = a conspicuous pause point
   - the end of sentence = an especially conspicuous pause point.

2.1 Reading out loud with pauses

4. Optional: highlight syllables that receive *exceptional* stress, e.g. by making them 'bold'.
5. Prepare to display the text in some fashion (e.g. on the board or on handouts).

in class

1. Hand out or display the text and give students time to read it.
2. Make sure the text is well understood.
3. Read it out dramatically, with all, and only, the pauses you have planned for. Although you may also wish to play a recording, students are likely to be more motivated if you read out the text *live* at some point.
4. Ask how the unusual layout of the text matches the way it was read out.
5. Let students hear the text again, the same way.
6. Repeat Step 5, breath group by breath group, with your class repeating each one after you (or after the recording). Both choral *and* individual repetition will be useful since it is important not to go on to the next step until you know that your students are ready to do it fairly well.
7. Ask students to take turns reading the text out to each other in pairs, *with pauses as previously indicated*. Circulate and help as needed.

Tips and Notes
- Using literary works is an option; but such works are not necessarily ideal for teaching everyday chunks since literary authors often try to avoid them.
- A good source of authentic materials is the BBC website: http://www.bbc.co.uk/radio/. There is also a children's section.
- Playing an excerpt from a recording of one of Martin Luther King's speeches can powerfully demonstrate the positive effect of good pausing. See, e.g., http://www.mlkonline.net/sounds.html

EXTENSION
To drive home the message that lexical chunks are *not* broken up by pauses, you could also first give a speech or tell a story with *unnatural* pauses, i.e. pauses *inside* chunks (e.g. *On the other // hand*; *When it comes // to …*; *I was // wondering if …*; *There's nothing new under // the sun*; *They're a rock band from down // under*), and ask students to identify what's wrong with your delivery.

2.2 Priming with Chinese whispers

> This short activity can be used to help students notice the wording of chunks that occur in a text which you plan to present to them – it is particularly suited to use as a pre-listening task before you play a recording of a song. It is probably *not* suitable for classes of more than 20 students.

Focus Any kind of chunk; warming up for listening to a song

Level Elementary–Intermediate

Time 5–10 minutes

Materials Slips of paper on which are written chunks from the lyrics of a song; a recording of the song (see p.102)

Preparation

1. Choose four multi-word bits from the song you are going to play. Each bit should be, or should contain, a common chunk. For example, from the Roy Orbison song 'Pretty Woman', you could choose: *Pretty woman, walking down the street; You look as lovely as can be; Don't make me cry; I'll treat you right* (see the examples). Choose one additional chunk in case you have to have some groups of five.

2. Write each of the four bits of song on a different slip of paper. When you've done that, you have a set for one group of four students. Make more sets of slips for as many groups as you will have. Make a few slips with your additional, fifth, line on them.

in class

1. Tell your class that:
   a) In a minute, they should divide up into standing groups of four or, if necessary, five.
   b) You will give everyone a slip of paper bearing a phrase or sentence which they should try to memorise. Circulate and answer questions about meaning and pronunciation.
   c) No one should show their slip to anyone else until the activity is finished.

2. Explain how Chinese Whispers works. (In other languages it may be called something like 'Broken Telephone'.) That is, in their groups, one student whispers the phrase to the person standing next to them on one side, who then whispers the phrase to the person standing next to them, who whispers it to the last person, who then must say what phrase s/he thinks s/he heard. The person who started off the chain of whispering tells and shows the others the phrase on the slip of paper. Every group member takes a turn whispering their phrase. Incidentally, it is probably a good idea to stipulate a maximum number of times that a whispered phrase can be repeated – three, perhaps.

3. Begin the activity. While it is in progress, write the words of the song title on the board, all jumbled up. For example, you could write 'Pretty Woman' as 'yretpt mwnao'

4. Ask the earliest finishers to try to solve the anagrammed title.

5. When everyone has finished, ask students from a group near the board to write up the phrases. Make sure everyone knows what they mean, and draw your students' attention to the commonest word combinations, e.g. by underlining them like this: *Pretty woman, walking down the street*.

6. Begin one of your normal procedures for using a recorded song. Students often give clear indication that they have paid particular attention to the phrases they met a few minutes earlier (in Steps 1–5).

Acknowledgement
We learned this application of Chinese Whispers from Randal Holme.

2.3 Memorising short dialogues

> This exercise, now undeservedly out of fashion, offers well motivated learners a means of memorising high frequency chunks – provided (but this is true of virtually all activities) that it is not used to excess.
>
> For learners at higher levels, a very effective extension of the basic idea is for them to perform plays, with each student memorising all of their character's lines as well as their cues (i.e. the lines spoken by other characters just before their own turn to speak).

Focus   Any kind of chunk; pronunciation

Level   Beginner–Pre-intermediate

Time   10 minutes in one lesson; 5–10 minutes in the next

Materials   A handout of a dialogue for each student, or a projectable copy (see p.103)

Preparation   Choose a very short dialogue containing one or more very high frequency chunks.

in class

1. Near the end of a lesson, present the dialogue. This is often done by playing a recording. When your students have heard it once or twice, ask them to guess the setting of each conversation and the relationship between the speakers. Then, line by line, clarify meaning, and conduct oral repetition drills in order to perfect pronunciation. At some stage, give your students the transcript to read. Their homework is to memorise the entire dialogue.

2. At the beginning of the next lesson, ask everyone to stand up, find two partners they do not usually work with, and sit or stand together somewhere in the room.

3. In each group, students one by one (try to) recite the dialogue. (The basic options are for each student to recite the whole thing or, which seems more natural, for pairs to recite it, each student taking a different role.) Partners may give each other hints as necessary.

4. Ask everyone to return to their previous seat.

5. Spot check students' recall.

Tip
Googling 'efl dialogues' and 'esl dialogs' turns up a large number of results – some of which are podcasts.

REVIEWING
Divide the class into small groups and ask them to try to remember and recite – or write down – a previously studied dialogue. Give them one of the lines as a prompt.

QUIZZING
Give students versions of previously learned dialogues (as in the examples) with key chunks gapped out; elicit the chunks from them.

2.3 - memorising at
home.

2. initials.

listen first - then.

write initials

prompt
'effortful recall
helps'

...nitials for?

...ge students first to listen for target chunks
...y for a short while before writing them
...e, students meet the target chunks in an
...ong lyrics.

...ntensive listening

...)4)

... words, including 4–8 chunks which you

...propriate for your class. (To the traditional
...ve added some chunks not in the original.)

...les - that is, put individual sentences/
...and replace each of the target chunks
...f your students.

in class **(for the example text)**

1. Begin with some discussion of the topic of the text. In the case of this text, see how many of Aesop's fables your students know, and see if anyone can tell you one or two of them all the way through. Then ask if anyone knows and can recount 'The Boy Who Cried Wolf'. Make sure they all know that in this case *crying out* means 'shouting' and is rather literary in tone.

2. Hand out copies of your worksheet and ask students to look through it and see if there are any words they want to ask about.

3. Then explain that:

   a) Now they must all put their pens or pencils down.

   b) Soon you will read out the text; and when you do, you will say all the words in full. Alternatively, you play a recording of the story or song with all the words spoken/sung in full.

   c) As soon as the story/song ends, students should pick up their pens and try to write the *full* wording (which they have just heard) near each set of initials.

4. Read out/play the full version of the story/lyrics.

5. Allow time for students to remember and write.

6. Ask everyone to compare their notes with a neighbour.

7. With the whole class, go through the story/lyrics from beginning to end, eliciting the full phrase for each set of initials.

REVIEWING/QUIZZING

It is easy to adapt this activity for the purpose of quizzing your students on their recall of chunks in a text that was used in some previous lesson:

1. Form pairs and give each pair one worksheet like the students' version of *The Boy Who Cried Wolf*.

2. Explain that partners should work together, talking in whispers, to try to remember, and write on the text sheet, the full wording for each set of initials. Allow everyone half a minute or so to remember all the phrases.

3. Then ask everyone to put down their pens.

4. Read out the full text fairly quickly.

5. Everyone can now pick up their pens and finish writing what they remember.

6. Collect the 'quiz sheets', or correct them in class.

Notes about using initials as memory prompts

In terms of learning and/or teaching, use of initials prompts has at least six potential benefits:

1. It requires a mental effort to recall a complete chunk with only its initials as a cue, and it is known that effortful recall helps entrench memory traces.

2. Use of initials draws students' attention to first letters and sounds. This is good because the beginnings of words are especially potent memory clues when you happen to have a meaning in mind and are searching through your memory for the matching word(s).

3. Initials highlight the number of words in any given chunk, which can also help each learner to successfully complete a mental word search.

4. Articles and other very small words are put on equal footing sizewise, which may help them to be noticed by learners whose mother tongues lack these kinds of words.

5. Initials take up little space, which makes it easier to fit a suitable text onto a projectable slide.

6. Making such hints requires no specialist knowledge.

2.5

Remember my change

In its rationale and procedure, this activity is similar to the previous one ('What are those initials for?'), but it is a little more challenging, and so the number of phrases targeted should be smaller (i.e. 2–5).

Focus Any kind of chunk

Level Upper elementary–Advanced

Time 15–30 minutes

Materials A handout for each student (for example texts, see p.105)

Preparation You need a text of 60–180 words suitable for your class. Edit it as necessary so as to create a student's version and a teacher's version. The latter should include 3–5 chunks which are missing from the former (see the examples). For example, you can create your students' version by eliminating chunks that are in the original text, which you then use as your teacher's version. Or you can create a teacher's version by adding chunks into an easy text (i.e. one you find in a coursebook).

in class

1. Generate some discussion around the topic of the text.
2. Ask students to read the text and make sure they understand it.
3. Say that you will read the text out loud but will make some changes to it as you do. Add that they should not write while you are reading and that as soon as you finish they should pick up their pens and add your changes into the text by writing new words or crossing out existing words, as necessary. Say also that they will get *two* chances to do this.
4. After two goes, ask students to compare their marked up texts.
5. Get everyone's attention, write the chunks on the board, and make sure everyone understands what the chunks mean and what register they are. For example, in the text 'The goose that laid golden eggs', students should know that *blood and guts* is colloquial and rather 'strong' whereas *insides* is a common euphemism for it.

REVIEWING

At the end of the lesson or the beginning of the next one:

1. Ask students to pair up.
2. Give each pair a fresh copy of the original students' version, and ask them *not* to try to find their old copies!
3. Ask them, from memory, to add into the story the same changes as you made before.
4. Check.

2.6 Writing then reconstructing

> This is a very simple and useful set of familiar but effective exercises. The main procedure involves students copying a text and then reconstructing it from memory with the help of prompts.

Focus   Any kind of chunk; intensive reading or listening; writing

Level   Beginner–Intermediate

Time   5–10 minutes

Materials   Several copies of a short text; a gapped version of the text for each student (or a projectable copy) based on the examples shown on p.106

Preparation

1. Make several copies of a short text containing useful chunks which you highlight. (See the examples).

2. Stick the copies up on the wall around your classroom. No student should have to walk very much farther than any other student does in order to reach one of the copies. If you have more than 25 or so students, see the Variation for Large Classes below.

PROCEDURE WITH COPYING

1. Explain that soon everyone should:

   a) get a sheet of paper and pen or pencil ready in front of them

   b) stand up and walk to one of the sheets of paper you have stuck on the wall

   c) remember as much of the beginning of the text as they can

   d) return to their seat and write what they remembered (but for names, they need only write initials)

   e) go back to the text, remember a bit more, write that down too, and so on – until they have copied all of the text correctly onto the sheet of paper on their desk

   f) highlight in their texts all the phrases that are highlighted in the texts on the wall.

2. Start the activity.

3. As students finish, ask them to turn their sheets over and see if they can write any of the highlighted phrases from memory.

4. When everyone has finished copying, read out or display the original so they can check their copy.

5. Give your class something completely different to do for five minutes or so. For instance, ask everyone to stand up and then lead a session of Simon Says. (This well known game is explained at: http://en.wikipedia.org/wiki/Simon_Says.)

6. Hand out copies of a severely gapped version of the text they copied before, and see if students can complete it individually or in pairs.

VARIATION FOR LARGE CLASSES

Steps 1–4: Instead of displaying the text on the walls, prepare a projectable slide. In class, ask everyone to put down their pens. Display the text; give everyone a chance to read it; check comprehension; explain that now everyone will have a chance to copy the text bit by bit starting with the beginning; turn off the display; ask students to write what they remember of the beginning; ask them to put down their pens; turn on the display again; and so on. If they want, allow students to work in pairs with one sheet of paper between them.

VARIATIONS WITH DICTATION (Elementary–Advanced)

Steps 1–2: Instead of copying the text before having to reconstruct it, students take it down from dictation in one of these ways:

1. Students-in-control dictation
    Dictate the text, but encourage students to ask questions and make requests – *What was that last bit again?, How do you spell ___?, What does ____ mean?* (This technique can be introduced into the two following variations.)

2. Basic mutual dictation
    Form pairs. Each partner has a different (part of a) text. Each dictates what they have to the other. Each checks what the other has written.

3. Running dictation
    This has much in common with copying a text off the wall, but here students are in pairs. One partner remains seated while the other goes to a text on the wall, remembers a bit, returns to his/her partner, dictates a bit of the text, goes back to the text in the wall, remembers a bit more, dictates that, and so on. (Partners can change roles halfway through the text.)

NOTE To learn more about the multi-faceted technique of dictation, see Davis and Rinvolucri (1988).

2.7 Filling in a story skeleton

> This exercise is designed to foster awareness of chunks, including ones commonly used to indicate the structure of a narrative.

Focus Any kind of chunk

Level Intermediate–Advanced

Time 45–60 minutes if done in one lesson

Materials A short gapped text to be displayed for all to see (for example, see p.107)

Preparation
1. Choose a short 'news-in-brief' newspaper article which includes some common chunks, as virtually all such articles do.
2. Gap the text (as shown in the examples) so as to leave only those words and chunks *which indicate the most basic gist and structure of the text*.

in class
1. Display the gapped text for all to see.
2. Ask everyone to copy it onto a sheet of paper so that it covers more or less one whole side. They do this mainly by making all the long gaps longer.
3. Read the original story out loud, paraphrasing potentially unfamiliar vocabulary as you go along. Then read it out at least one more time. *During this step, your students only listen.*
4. Students each fill in the gaps to make a newspaper-like story.
5. In small groups, students read their completed texts to each other.
6. Hide the gapped text and ask everyone to turn over their stories.
7. Give everyone a copy of the original text and ask them, working individually, to underline or highlight *only* the words that appeared on the gapped text sheet.
8. Ask students to form pairs and compare what they've marked.
9. Display the gapped text again.

Note

If you ask students to do Step 4 at home, Steps 5–9 should be done in the following lesson.

Dicto-composition:
from chunks to text and back

> This is a variation of the well known exercise which is often, but inscrutably, called a 'dictogloss'. In doing it, students listen intensively to a spoken text, take notes, and then expand their notes, in writing, into a text resembling the original version as much as possible. The aim in our variation is to focus as sharply as possible on a contextualised set of target chunks, which can be of any type. It is most suitable for classes of well motivated students.

Focus   Any kind of chunk; intensive listening; writing

Level   Upper elementary–Advanced

Time   20–40 minutes, depending on the text

Materials   A class set of a text (for example, see below)

Preparation

1. Choose a text (50–120 words or so) to read out to the class. The text should contain several conventional word combinations. Or you could use the example below.

2. If you choose a different text, mark each combination as in the passage below, where Nelson Mandela is describing his life in South Africa as a political (as opposed to a common, or 'common law') prisoner.

> "Although our work at the quarry <u>was meant to</u> show us that we were <u>no different from the other</u> prisoners, the authorities still <u>treated us like</u> the <u>lepers</u> who once populated the island. Sometimes we would see a group of common-law prisoners working <u>by the side of the road</u>, and their warders would order them into the bushes so they would not see us <u>as we marched past</u>. <u>It was as if</u> the mere <u>sight of</u> us might somehow affect their discipline. Sometimes <u>out of the corner of an eye</u> we could see a prisoner <u>raise his fist</u> in the ANC salute."
>
> Nelson Mandela. ***Long Walk to Freedom***. London: Abacus, p. 480

in class

1. Down the centre of the board, write what you judge to be the most worthwhile chunks to focus on – like this example, but with plenty of room between the lines:

was meant to

no different from the other

treated us like …lepers

by the side of the road

as we marched past.

It was as if

out of the corner of an eye

2. Make sure your students understand what each chunk means, and then ask everyone to copy what's on the board onto a blank sheet of paper.

3. Out loud, slowly read the whole of the text containing the chunks. Explain unfamiliar vocabulary as you go along and afterwards check your students' understanding of the text as a whole.

4. Explain that you will read the text out again and that as you do so they should add onto their papers as much of the rest of the text as they can.

5. As you read the text out, circulate to see how well your students are managing.

6. Ask students to form pairs. Add that one person in each pair should be 'secretary' and do all the writing. Explain that each pair should work *as a team* and try to write a text as close as possible to the one you dictated. Stress that whenever they cannot remember the exact words, they should try to express the relevant meaning in good English but in their own words.

7. Ask a few secretaries to read out their texts. Other secretaries listen and add improvements to their texts.

8. Hand out or display the original for purposes of comparison.

9. At the end of the lesson, ask partners to try to remember the phrases they copied off the board.

EXTENSION

For homework, or in a later lesson, ask students to incorporate the chunks into a story of their own invention. Suggest a few titles/settings (e.g. *My years in an English boarding school*, *Taken hostage!*, *A party that turned into a nightmare*), but allow students to choose their own title if they want to. Encourage them to use the chunks in an order different from that given above.

Tips

Re Step 5: obviously, in order to compose a full text, students must have reasonably complete notes. On the other hand, if their notes are too close to the original, that can undercut your goal of getting them to engage in effortful recall during the following composition activity. Adjust both your reading speed and the number of times you read out the text so as to avoid this risk. When you see that some students have good notes, instead of you reading out the whole text, ask one or more of these students to read out what they have written down.

Re Step 6: Ideally, the secretary should be the person in the pair who has the *least* complete notes at this point, otherwise the student with the more complete notes may just start writing without asking for help from the other.

REVIEWING

Display a version of the text with these phrases gapped out (see p.107), and ask students, in pairs or threes, to list the target phrases in the order they occur.

Questionnaires with multiple choice answers

> One aim of this activity is to get students talking about themselves. Another is to rehearse chunks that are included within a set of scripted questions and/or a set of recommended answers.

Focus Chunks such as expressions of frequency (*all the time*), time of day (*in the evening*), actions (*have breakfast*), chunks which can begin a question (*When do you…?*); guided speaking; getting better acquainted with a partner

Level Upper elementary–Pre-intermediate

Time 20–40 minutes

Materials A class set of each of the two handouts (see p.108). The smaller handout can instead be dictated or displayed as a slide.

Preparation
1. Adapt either of the handouts as appropriate for your class or make new handouts to practise different chunks.
2. Sheet 1: Prepare a slide or a class set of photocopies, or prepare to dictate it.
3. Sheet 2: Make *half* a class set and then divide each handout in two. In pairs, each student will get a different half.

in class

PROCEDURE
1. Hand out, display or dictate Sheet 1 and check for understanding.
2. Write some questions on the board, e.g:
   When do you brush your teeth? / When do you sleep? / breathe?
3. Ask three students each to ask you one of the questions. Answer them using expressions in Sheet 1.
4. Form A–B pairs; give student A in each pair a copy of the top half of Sheet 2, and ask the As to interview the Bs by asking those questions. Add that:
   - the Bs, after they answer, should ask, "And you?"
   - the Bs should try to use the answers on Sheet 1.
   - the As should, in general, not *show* the questions to their partners.
5. When the As have asked all their questions, give the Bs the bottom half of Sheet 2 so that they can now interview the As. The reason that the Bs get new questions is so that the As can also have the experience of answering unexpected questions.
6. When the interviews are finished, ask everyone to hide their copies of Sheet 1. In pairs, they should write down all the expressions they remember from Sheet 1 (i.e., all the time and frequency expressions).

VARIATIONS
- Compose questions that repeatedly include other chunks, e.g. *How long does it take the earth to go around the sun?*; *How long does it take you to write out your full name?*; *Could you tell me where your driving licence is now?*, *Could you tell me what you keep under your bed?*
- Provide only the questions – not the answers.

2.10 Between-listening gap fills

In this sequence of exercises, students first do jigsaw listening (see the explanation below). Following that, they try to fill in a gapped transcript based on both parts of the listening material. Then they hear both parts of the listening material, including the part which only their partner had heard before. The inclusion of the gap filling activity between the two listening stages gives students – now that they are not having to concentrate so intently on listening – the opportunity (a) to evaluate each other's reports, (b) to satisfy curiosity about things that were left unclear in the report given by their partners, and (c) to have a closer look at useful language, especially chunks.

To do a jigsaw listening exercise, you need to split the class into two groups. Each group then listens to a different but related recording or perhaps different halves of the same recording. After listening, learners who have listened to different material join up in pairs and tell each other about the contents of their part.

Focus   Any kind of chunk; intensive reading; preparation for listening

Level   Intermediate–Advanced

Time   50–60 minutes; can be done over two lessons

Materials   Recording(s) of TV or radio programme(s); two tape/CD/DVD players (unless you have access to a language laboratory or multimedia room); gapped transcript of the recordings (for example, see p.109)

Preparation   1. Prepare two recordings: either two different programmes about the same theme which complement one another information-wise, or two copies of the same programme that can be split in half without each half becoming incomprehensible.

2. Prepare for the split class context, either by reserving two rooms (one for each of the tape/CD/DVD players) or by setting up the recordings in the language laboratory / multimedia room.

3. Create a gapped transcript by deleting words which are *guessable* because they are part of common chunks and are preceded by cues. Make sure you include a good number of chunks that your students are already familiar with (at least receptively), so that they will (a) benefit from the positive result of their successful guessing and (b) gain positive evidence that knowledge of chunks makes it easier to achieve detailed understanding of challenging spoken texts.

in class   1. Check that everyone knows how a jigsaw listening exercise works. It might also be a good idea to check that they know what kind of notes to take and also to give them an idea of how detailed (or how long) their eventual oral report to their partners should be when they exchange information about their texts in Step 3.

2. Students listen to their assigned text.

3. In pairs or threes, students report to each other what they heard in their different texts.

4. Hand out the gapped transcript(s). Students can work in the same pairs or threes to try to fill in the blanks.

5. Tell everyone they will now get the opportunity to listen to *both* recordings with the support of their (fully or partly) filled in gapped transcripts. Add that they should listen with a view to evaluating both their own and their partners' reports.

6. Play the recording(s) again so students can check their work on the gap-fill task.

7. Allow time for the students to talk about the completeness and accuracy of the oral reports they gave in Step 3.

Teach your phrase

> This is a jigsaw reading and speaking activity that incorporates a stage in which students teach chunks to each other. The rationale for this stage is not so much that students will durably remember the chunks that other students teach them but that they should remember the one they try to teach to others.

Focus Figurative idioms, clichés, proverbs, common collocations, discourse markers, functional exponents; reading; speaking

Level Pre-intermediate–Advanced

Time 10–30 minutes

Materials Copies of several very short storylike texts (as on pp.110-113); enough good dictionaries

Preparation

1. Find or compose a number of short texts such that each text contains a chunk that you want your students to learn. It is very important that the context should give strong clues about the meaning of each target chunk.

2. Highlight the target chunks (e.g. by underlining); and optionally (depending on the level of your learners) add some text-comprehension questions and at least one 'concept' question (i.e. a question intended to guide students toward correct understanding of the target chunk).

3. Make enough copies of each text (see examples).

in class

1. Divide your class into groups of four or so. Give each student in a group a copy of the same text, and give different texts to different groups.

2. Explain that everyone should read their text and then check with the others in their group that they correctly understand both their text and their target chunk. For this, encourage the use of a good dictionary of idioms and/or phrasal verbs.

3. As groups are working, circulate and make sure that each group is on the right track about the meaning of their text and their chunk.

4. As groups finish, explain that soon everyone will be in a new group consisting of members who have each read a different text with a different target chunk in it. Say that before they all change to a new group you are going to give them more time, in their *present* group, to practise (a) telling their text out loud *from memory* (although not necessarily word-perfect) and (b) teaching their target chunk clearly *in English* – because that's what they will have to do when they change groups.

5. Circulate while the groups are practising.

6. Form the new groups in which everyone has a different text, and recommend the following order of presentation: one by one, each student tells their story, then teaches their chunk, and then tells their story again. Then it's the turn of another student, and so on.

7. As groups finish, ask the members of each group to swap texts, read them, and note down the different target chunks in their notebooks along with indications of meaning (e.g. a translation) and hints about how to use it (e.g. they include it in a complete, explanatory sentence or in a little dialogue).

Ask some of your students how they have recorded the new chunks in their notebooks, and give tips about how to improve such notes.

VARIATIONS

Students may –

1. work in pairs, in which case each partner might have more than one text to read and/or more than one chunk to teach.

2. choose for themselves what chunks to teach.

Phrasal verbs via paired associates

One reason why phrasal verbs are relatively hard to understand and remember is that it is often difficult, if not impossible, to find accurate synonyms or translations. Another problem is that the same few verbs and prepositions tend to occur over and over again in different combinations, which makes it easy for learners to become confused about which phrasal verb has what meaning.

Fortunately, a number of recently published learners' dictionaries deal very well with meaning and usage of common phrasal verbs, and materials for home study of phrasal verbs have improved in the same respect. But the problem of how learners can *remember* phrasal verbs remains. Here we describe a version of the tried and tested 'associated pairs' technique which can be used to focus on particular phrasal verbs so persistently that these verbs should finally come quickly to mind when they are needed.

Focus   Verb+preposition+object phrasal verbs

Level   Pre-intermediate–Advanced

Time   Variable

Materials   None for the main procedure

Preparation

1. Choose a small set of phrasal verbs to work on – or ask your students to look through their notes and suggest ones that they understand but just can't seem to remember well enough to use. In order to make your students' job easier, avoid simultaneous focus on phrases that have the same main verb. Try also to avoid too much repetition of the same preposition, especially if they have rather different meanings/functions (e.g. *take up (a new hobby), make up (with sb)…*).

2. For each phrasal verb you select, choose a sentence that represents a common usage. A dictionary of phrasal verbs could be a big help here. A bonus offered by some of these dictionaries is that they tell you which phrasal verbs are especially frequent and therefore especially worth focusing on. Let's take the phrasal verb *pull (s'thing) off* as an example. The *Oxford Phrasal Verbs Dictionary for Learners of English* (2006) gives the following examples – *She pulled off her hat and gloves* and *The goalie pulled off a terrific save.* The former, which is distinctly literal, could be a target at pre-intermediate level. The latter, which is distinctly idiomatic, is a target for intermediate level or above.

3. Edit or adapt the example sentences as appropriate. For example, we would shorten *She pulled off her hat and gloves* to *She pulled off her gloves*. The second example, about the goalie, seems good as it is.

4. Write up your list of examples as shown on the next page.

Pre-intermediate	**Paired associates**
She pulled off her gloves.	pull off // gloves
Look these words up in your dictionary.	look up // words
Put away your toys!	put away // toys
While cleaning the attic, she came across. an old photo	come across // an old photo

Intermediate–advanced	**Paired associates**
The goalie pulled off a terrific save.	pull off // a terrific save
She always looked up to her older sister.	look up to // older sister
Put me down for a ticket. I'll pay later.	put me down for // a ticket
The government has come in for severe criticism.	come in for // criticism

in class

1. Write your example sentences and paired associates (see above) on the board, and make sure that everyone knows what each sentence and each phrasal verb means.

2. Ask everyone to start a special 'phrasal verb' section in their notebooks. It should include the lists you have put on the board.

3. Say that you are going to try to help them remember phrasal verbs, set by set, with a new set being added in every other lesson (or once a week or whatever you decide). Explain that their job is to remember, first of all, the paired associates and also – but more *in the back of their minds* – the matching sentences that they come from.

4. Later in the lesson, after asking students **not** to look at their notes, write up your paired associates in jumbled fashion and ask how they should be matched. Then ask who can remember the sentence each paired associate goes with.

REVIEWING

From time to time in the same and in later lessons, review as follows:

- Read out the first part of one of the example sentences and see if anyone can finish it.

- Write up clues such as *p. off // a terrific s.*, and elicit the full paired associates. Afterwards, see if anyone can remember the matching sentences more or less faithfully.

- Call out a phrasal verb and see if anyone can call out the associate or, which is harder, do the reverse.

- Ask students to quiz each other in small groups. That is, one – in the role of teacher – looks at their list of sentences and paired associates and calls out hints and prompts, e.g. "About her older sister … the younger sister always looked …".

QUIZZING

When given one associate and a hint (e.g. initials), students must supply the other: e.g. "Write the missing word(s): *pull off //* ➔ *a t. s.* ...."

Putting chunks into chronological order: romantic relationships

> This sequence of activities exploits the fact that many kinds of words and phrases become easier to remember when chronologically ordered and/or included in narrative.

Focus Figurative idioms, phrasal verbs; writing & reading out stories

Level Pre-intermediate–Upper intermediate

Time 1–1½ hours over one or two lessons

Materials A slide or class set of handouts (see p.113)

Preparation Prepare a handout (or slide display) of the jumbled sentences

in class

1. Elicit/explain what a 'chat-up' line is. (It's what someone says in the hope that they can attract the attention of someone they find interesting.)

2. One at a time, dictate (some of) the following chat-up lines.

a Excuse me. I've lost my phone number. Can I have yours?
b Hi, I'm Mr Right. Someone said you were looking for me.
c You must be exhausted 'cause you've been running through my mind all night.
d It's your lucky day – my girlfriend dumped me last night.
e Did it hurt . ..when you fell down from heaven?
f Was your father a thief? No, well, who stole the stars and put them in your eyes?
g Life is a jigsaw puzzle, and for me you are the missing piece.
h Your eyes are the same colour as my Porsche.
i If I could rearrange the alphabet, I would put U and I together.
j I must be lost. I thought Paradise was further south.
k I'm not really this tall. I'm sitting on my wallet.
l There's something wrong with my phone. It doesn't have your number in it.
m Can I borrow 20p? I promised my mother I'd phone her if I fell in love.
n If you were a hamburger, you'd be a McGorgeous!
o I think I saw you in the dictionary next to 'WooOoo!"

3. Ask students to form groups of three or so and talk about how successful these lines might be and what kind of person might say them. Ask them also to mention any other chat-up lines they might know, including ones which girls or women might use.

4. Ask them to look at the chat-up lines they have written and get ready to underline the particular phrases which you are going to read out. Then read out, in jumbled order, whichever of the following word combinations are in the chat-up lines you've used:

2.13 Putting chunks into chronological order: romantic relationships

a) *Excuse me, I've lost my …, Can I have …?;*

b) *looking for;*

c) *You must be exhausted, running through my mind;*

d) *It's your lucky day, my girlfriend dumped me;*

e) *Did it hurt … ?;*

f) *the missing piece;*

g) *the same colour as;*

h) *If I could …, I would …;*

i) *not really;*

k) *There's something wrong with my…;*

l) *Can I borrow …?, I promised … I'd …, fell in love;*

m) *If you were …, you'd …;*

n) *I think I saw you ….*

For example, if chat-up line (a), *Excuse me*, comes first in the list you gave your students, don't start with it. Read it out later on, to make your students hunt around a bit.

5. Ask your students to turn their papers over and each tell a neighbour any chat-up lines they remember.

6. Optional: on a handout (or by some other means), present the jumbled sentences (in examples), and see who can guess what the idioms mean.

7. Ask your students to work individually or in pairs, as they prefer, to re-order the jumbled sentences by writing them out completely, in chronological order, so as to make a typical story. They don't need to include the glosses which are given at the ends of some of the sentences.

8. Invite a few students to read their stories out to the class.

9. Ask students to turn their papers over so that they can't look at their sentences and stories.

REVIEWING

1. Dictate the phrases given just below, and ask students, individually or in pairs, to put them in a plausible chronological order (not necessarily the same as before):

make up	have a row	fall in love
pop the question	break off their engagement	hit it off
tie the knot	catch … eye	set a date for
hang out together	get on	so far so good
chat … up	be engaged to be married	

2. Ask everyone to write another story, in complete sentences, using the phrases as they ordered them in Step 1 just above. This time, though, they add details that were not in the earlier story – e.g. places, names, descriptions, a plot that is somehow different, a chat-up line and a reply, and so on.

3. As students finish their stories, ask them to join up with others who have finished and to read their stories to each other while other students are still finishing. As the last students finish, they join an existing group and read out their stories too.

Tip
Perhaps begin or end the sequence of activities by using a romantic song – e.g. 'It's now or never' by Elvis Presley.

2.14 Situational clichés

This sequence of exercises targets situation-bound clichés such as *The more the merrier* and *Small world!* With advanced classes of adult learners, we have worked with as many as three dozen clichés at once (because every advanced level participant will know a lot of them already). At lower levels, however, you will certainly want to target fewer expressions than that, which you can do by deleting items from the handout.

Focus Fixed expressions like *Small world!*; writing dialogues and reading them

Level Pre-intermediate–Advanced

Time 30–40 minutes for the basic procedure; 44–50 minutes for the extension

Materials A sheet of paper per student; copies/a projection of worksheets (see p.116)

Preparation
1. Choose some clichés and produce a master list like the one shown on pp.114-115.

2. Then make two differently gapped versions of your master copy. So each version should lack some of the explanations (and a couple of the clichés). But any deleted information must be present in the other version. Let us call these two versions Sheet A and Sheet B. Produce enough A & B sheets so that one student in each pair will get the A sheet and the other the B sheet.

3. For reviewing, prepare a projectable display of the Initials Prompts; see Reviewing Step 2.

in class
1. Form pairs and distribute the A and B sheets.

2. Explain that everyone should read all their clichés and all the explanations that they have on their sheet. Add that if any information or any cliché is missing from their sheet, they must ask their partner to tell them what it is. Their job then is simply to write this explanation down onto their own sheet.

3. While students are exchanging information, go to the board and write up the initials of each of the target chunks – e.g. for *Fingers crossed!* write *F. c !* Be creative with colour, style and layout – i.e., do not put the initials in ordered rows and columns.

4. As pairs finish, invite them to come to the board to see how many of the initials they can 'translate' into the corresponding full phrase. (One purpose of this step is to give early finishers of Step 2 something fruitful to do while the others are still working.)

5. When everyone has completed their sheet, ask everyone who is standing to sit down, and then test the whole class by pointing to each of the initials in turn. Whoever remembers the corresponding phrase can call it out.

6. Form the class into new pairs or threes. They all look at the initials on the board and try to remember them all, with partners helping each other.

EXTENSION

7. Form pairs; each student to have a full-size sheet of paper.

8. Everyone prepares their sheet as follows (see also the example):

   a) They draw a vertical line or make a crease down the centre.

   b) They draw a box, top centre, in which they mention two people and the situation or place they are in.

   c) They choose a cliché that was new for them and write it at the top of the left side of their paper, e.g. *It takes two to tango*. This cliché is supposed to be something that one of the people mentioned in their box has just said.

   d) At the top they should indicate which of the two people in fact said this (e.g. 'the woman').

9. Partners exchange papers. Each must now take on the role indicated on their partner's sheet (i.e., they are the second person mentioned in the box) and write an appropriate response to what the first person said (e.g., "You don't think I had anything to do with it do you?"). At this point students should *not* try to use another one of the clichés, as doing so would probably make it too difficult to continue a plausible dialogue.

10. They continue to exchange papers, writing replies to each other's replies, e.g., "I don't think she would've kissed you with no encouragement from you!"

11. After 20–30 minutes ask everyone to bring their dialogues to a close.

12. Form pairs into groups of 6–8 students so that everyone can have an audience as they recite their two dialogues. If you think the dialogues may need editing, collect them and leave this step for the next lesson.

Tip

Re Step 3: In your initials, retain hyphens and apostrophes, and put a full stop after each abbreviated letter, but not after the article *a*. Thus, *I'm having a senior moment* becomes *I' h. a s. m.* You can make certain phrases easier to recall by adding more letters, e.g. *I'm h. a se. mo.*

REVIEWING

1. Ask students to find their original worksheets and fold them so they can only see the explanations. In pairs or threes they try to remember as many of the matching clichés as they can.

2. Form trios or fours. In each group give one student, preferably the least confident, a review sheet like the Review Prompts Sheet. The student with this sheet tests the other group members, giving hints as necessary.

QUIZZING

Give out another version of the original list; on each line, either the cliché or the explanation is missing, and students must fill in the blanks. Or re-use the review prompts sheet, this time as a quiz sheet.

Note

This approach also works with proverbs.

Acknowledgement

We learned the writing activity from Christine Frank and Mario Rinvolucri.

CHAPTER 3
TEACHING SETS OF CHUNKS: HELPING STUDENTS REMEMBER THEM

Introduction

This chapter builds on Chapter 2 by demonstrating how to:

- facilitate chunk-learning within a communicative, integrated-skills approach.
- encourage students to engage in the kinds of rich mental processing that are especially likely to result in the formation of robust memories for chunks of language.

A key element of this work is using 'linguistic motivation' to make chunks easier to remember (see pp. 12-13).

In order to demonstrate a good range of techniques and procedures, we have tried to avoid making each activity sequence like all the others. Regarding running time, we have expected that some teachers might sometimes prefer to use a short sequence of activities instead of one long activity, or vice versa. Regarding lesson structure, we have noticed that while most students appreciate variation, some require it in order to stay interested.

You will probably want to adapt this material to suit the particular needs and interests of your own students and the requirements of your teaching. For example, you may decide to pitch a worksheet to a lower level of learner by deleting some of the chunks that it includes. It is also possible to raise the level of the materials given here by, for instance, adding chunks.

The topic areas that figure in this chapter are ones that we have settled on for one or another of the following reasons:

- The topic area commonly crops up in official syllabuses.
- It embraces a number of chunks that are relatively frequent, relatively learnable, and relatively memorable (e.g. 3.3, 'Figurative manner-of-action expressions').
- It is a topic which, in our experience, teenagers and young adults can get interested in (all the units).
- It affords useful insights into Anglophone (especially British) culture and history (e.g. 3.7, 'Seafaring idioms' and 3.10, 'Horse-related idioms').

Of course, *all the chunks you target will need to be reviewed* so it is important to keep a record of chunks you want to come back to later – for Activity 3.17, ones with word repetition, rhyme, consonance, alliteration and assonance. For more ideas about how do this, see Chapter 4.

Remember that for each activity you want to prepare, when you read through the text for the first time you will need to have to hand a photocopy of the relevant worksheets, so that you can fully understand how that activity works.

3.1 Things that smell

> Under the umbrella of 'smells', this sequence of activities focuses on compound nouns (e.g. *hand lotion, rainforest*), other modifier + noun chunks (e.g. *an outdoor barbecue*), verbal chunks (e.g. *smells of, reminds me of, I associate__ with __*) and also a few whole-sentence chunks such as *That does nothing for me.*

Focus Chunks related to the topic of smells; speaking; listening

Level Pre-intermediate +

Time 40 minutes

Materials Copies of the handouts on pp.117 and 118

Preparation Find and bring to class a few things with strong but pleasant smells, such as samples of herbs (e.g. rosemary, lavender, mint, bay leaf), spices (especially cloves and cinnamon), pieces of fragrant soap, bits of perfumed paper, throat lozenges and so on. (As some students may be allergic to petrochemical-based scents, avoid commercial scent diffusers etc.)

in class

1. **Optional:** elicit names of herbs and spices. Ask also what parts of a plant each one tends to come from. (Herbs tend to consist of the softer or finer parts of plants such as leaves and flowers, whereas spices tend to consist of harder, coarser parts, such as seeds and bark, which may be ground into a powder.)

2. Form A/B pairs. Tell all the Bs to close their eyes.

3. Give each A student a sample of one of your smelly materials.

4. Ask the As to pass their sample (first crushing it if necessary) under the nose of their partner who, *only in whispers*, should try to guess what it is.

5. After a while, see who knows what the sample is, and write the word for it up on the board.

6. Repeat with the other samples, alternating between Bs and As.

7. Form pairs and give each partner a different section of the List of Things that Smell. At pre-intermediate level, 15 items per student is about right; at advanced level, divide the whole list between partners. Also, give each partner a copy of the Responses Sheet.

8. Ask students, in their pairs, to take turns reading the expressions on the lists out loud. Add that when one partner reads out an expression, the other partner(s) *must* respond in some way – either in brief or at length – according to their feeling about the smell in question. They may use the Possible Responses Sheet in the examples as a guide.

9. Ask early finishers to come to the board and, from memory, write up smelly things that they remember from the list.

EXTENSION

10. As appropriate to the level of your students, introduce a few figurative uses of smell vocabulary – e.g. *That stinks!* (= is terrible); *When he criticised her dress, she replied with a few pungent* (= not mild) *comments of her own; There's something fishy* (= smelly = suspicious) *about his behaviour; There's something rotten in the state of Denmark* (= *something isn't* right about this situation; from *Hamlet*); *Has she caught wind* (= catch a smell carried on the wind) *of the surprise party we're planning for her?; He is a master of distraction by using red herrings* (sb being tracked by bloodhounds could distract them, apparently, by dropping red (i.e. smoked) fish on the ground so as to send the dogs off in a different direction).

3.2 Things that make sounds

> This activity is designed to present and lightly entrench chunks and collocations that have to do with things that produce sounds. Deeper entrenchment can be facilitated by using the review and quiz activities described in Chapter 4.

Focus   Chunks related to the topic of sounds; speaking; listening

Level   Intermediate +

Time   40 minutes for the main sequence

Materials   One copy of the Personal Reactions Sheet, and half of the List of Sounds, for each student (see p.119)

Preparation   Be sure that you can explain the meaning of *onomatopoeia*!

in class

1. Ask everyone to close their eyes for ten seconds or so and just listen.
2. Ask your students what they have heard.
3. **Optional:** talk briefly about John Cage's 4'33", a short musical composition whose three movements are each completely silent even though musicians are on the stage as if ready to play it. Ask your students what they think a concert audience hears while that piece is being 'performed'.
4. **Optional:** clarify the typical difference in meaning between e.g. *I heard someone speak* and *I heard someone speaking*.
5. Form pairs (A & B), and give each partner a different section of the list of sounds in the examples. Allow everyone time to read and understand all their phrases and also to rate each phrase on their own list from +5 to -5, depending how positive or negative the sound is for them *for any reason* (with 0 signifying 'neutral').
6. Give everyone a copy of the Personal Reactions Sheet.
7. Explain that soon they will be reading their lists to each other out loud as follows:
   a) A slowly and theatrically reads out all her/his sound phrases.
   b) After hearing each one, B must respond, by using, if he/she wants, one of the expressions on the Personal Reactions Sheet.
   c) A should tell B whenever she/he notices a strong similarity or difference between how the two of them feel about a sound.
8. Ask early finishers to come to the board and, from memory, write up as many of the phrases as they can remember.
9. Ask if they can think of any other common sounds that could be on the list.
10. Elicit or give a definition of onomatopoeia (in a fairly broad sense) and ask your class what examples of onomatopoeia they see on the list of sounds.

EXTENSION

11. Invite students to compare onomatopoeic animal sounds in English (L$_2$) and in their mother tongue(s) (L$_1$). What cases do they know that are very similar? A bit similar? Apparently different?

12. In higher-level classes, introduce figurative idioms such as those listed here, and invite students to guess their meanings:

- *He's a ticking time bomb.*
- *The results of that experiment set alarm bells ringing.*
- *On the calendar it says we have an appointment with our lawyer tomorrow. Does that ring a bell with you?*
- *She likes to trumpet her own successes.*
- *February 29th, by custom, is the day that women can pop the question.*
- *He won't win the election unless he can drum up more support.* (This comes from the old practice of military recruitment being carried out with the aid of drummers marching through the streets.)

REVIEWING

Later in the same lesson or at the beginning of the next one, form groups of four or five. In each group, one student (the 'teacher') has the complete original Sounds list. The other students call out phrases which they think were on the list or could have been on it. The teacher' replies to each suggestion with "On the list" or "Not on the list" and also with a correction whenever a phrase that is on the list has been inaccurately formed by the person who called it out. When expressions stop coming, the 'teacher' calls out key words of the remaining phrases (e.g. *Sheep*) in hope that one of the other students will remember *Sheep baaing* or *Baaing sheep*. After a decent interval, call time and ask the 'teachers' to read out to their groups the phrases that no one remembered.

3.3 Figurative manner-of-action expressions

> This unit is designed to:
> - firmly entrench knowledge of a number of manner-of-action words (e.g. *snap*)
> - familiarise students with chunks in which these words are used figuratively (e.g. *a snap decision*).
>
> As usual, your choice of target verbs and chunks will depend on the level of your students.

Focus Manner-of-action verbs in literal and figurative chunks; standing up and moving as a brief change of pace; inferring meanings

Level Pre-intermediate +

Time 3–30 minutes per lesson, depending on the activity

Materials **Optional:** a handout of figurative examples (see pp.120-121)

Preparation
1. Choose a dozen or so manner-of-action verbs which are used figuratively in well-known chunks – e.g. 'dodge' in *dodge a question*.
2. For all or most of the verbs you've chosen, think of how to use it literally in a phrase – e.g. *lean left, step back, pick up a pen, put it down, turn it around, turn over your notebook, blow on your hands, touch your nose, stroke your wrist, pat your own back, click*UK*/snap*US *your fingers, swing your arms, dodge an imaginary tomato, wriggle like a worm, spin around, sway like bamboo in the wind, scratch your head, rub your hands together, flick an imaginary mosquito off your wrist*. Learners' dictionaries, and online concordance samplers – e.g. the Collins Cobuild Concordance Sampler: www.collins.co.uk/corpus/corpussearch.aspx – are a good source of information about both literal and figurative uses.

in class
1. Over the next two or three lessons, whenever your students look as though they might benefit from a bit of moving around, ask them to stand up and imitate your movements each time you call out one of the verb phrases you have selected..
2. Call out a series of commands, perform the corresponding actions, and encourage your students to join in.
3. Eventually, when students have had several commands, ask them to form groups of five or so. They take turns calling out a command which the others should carry out. Or students take turns performing actions which their partners should try to put into words.
4. When your students have learned one set of action expressions fairly well, show how a few (not necessarily all) of these expressions can be used figuratively. For example, display a set of figurative examples on the board, or provide them on a handout (see examples).
5. Form pairs and ask partners to consider the examples one by one to see if they can agree about a possible meaning of each highlighted expression.
6. Call the class together and go through the list example by example. Each time see if anyone in the class can give a good paraphrase (or translation) of the highlighted expression.

3.4 Weather phrases

> This short sequence of activities can be a useful supplement to a broader sequence of work on the topic of climate and weather. It begins with consideration of weather phrases used literally, and finishes with exploration of some of their metaphorical usages.

Focus Chunks having to do with weather

Level Intermediate +

Time 50 minutes

Materials Class sets of the worksheet (see p.122), and the List of Example Sentences (p.123)

Preparation Make class sets of the handouts.

in class

1. Give each of your students a copy of the worksheet, and make sure they understand each of the words and phrases in the left-hand column. (The difference between mist and haze is that mist is associated with humidity and haze with airborne dust, thin smoke and pollution. And just in case you get asked, fog is thick mist, the definition being that visibility is less than 100 metres.)

2. Ask students to pair up and help each other fill in each of the boxes in the Advantage and Disadvantage columns. In doing this, they should concentrate especially on the weather words (e.g. **rainy, frost, chilly wind ...**) rather than on more general vocabulary such as **day, heavy, morning, slight** and so on. Although partners work together, each should fill in their own sheet.

3. Ask students, keeping their worksheets, to form groups of four or five (partners from Step 2 should not be in the same group), and compare ideas.

4. Ask everyone to resume their original seat. For some or all of the weather conditions, ask what advantages and disadvantages they've thought of. (For some items, it may take considerable ingenuity to think of an advantage.)

5. Ask them to turn over their worksheets. Call out a key word from each phrase in the left-hand column (e.g. 'heavy') and see if anyone in the class can call out the whole phrase ('A heavy frost').

6. Call the class together, hand out the List of Example Sentences and ask pairs to go through the sentences one by one to see if they can agree about the meaning of each one. In particular, they should ask themselves (and each other) "How does the meaning we think this phrase has here relate to the basic 'weather meaning' of the key weather word?"

7. Call the class together again and quickly check that all the sentences have been correctly understood.

3.4 Weather phrases

Language notes

- re *bright* and *breezy*: words having to do with light are often used about understanding and being clever (e.g. **Aha! that's clear to me now**, **Can you clarify that for me?, Can you throw any light on the matter?, She's very bright**).Also, we say that a smile is bright. So here **bright** means both 'cheerful' and 'smart, alert', and **breezy** suggests 'fresh' and 'active'.

- re: **blue sky thinking**: To look at the sky, we must look up. A blue sky occurs on a sunny day, and we think of the sky as a place without limits. Therefore, 'blue sky thinking' is confident and optimistic, and goes beyond normal limits.

3.5

Device idioms

> This sequence of speaking and thinking activities again shows how idioms can be effectively taught by starting with literal meanings and then moving on to figurative meanings. Here, most of the key words designate hand tools (e.g. **axe**) although some designate other kinds of device or functional object (e.g. **comb**).

Focus Figurative idioms containing device nouns such as **axe;** speaking; inferring meanings

Level Upper intermediate +

Time 40–50 minutes to work on the literal meanings; 25–30 minutes to work on the figurative expressions (not counting Step 12); if target words are added, the whole sequence will last longer

Materials Handouts: word lists (see below), Review Sheet and Figurative Idioms Sheet (p.124); also dictionaries

Preparation Make a class set of two different lists of device words, for example, one list could have a spade, sieve, rake, belt, sledgehammer, comb, barbed wire; the other list could have axe, screw, oar, hourglass, door mat, wedge, funnel. The lists include only device words that occur in well-known figurative expressions. If you wish to use this activity more for fluency practice than for chunk teaching, include on your lists other/additional words such as: (intermediate) **spoon, knife, bowl, hairbrush, scarf ...** (upper intermediate) **saw, nail file, mittens ...;** (advanced) **colander, easel, ice-scraper ...**

in class

1. **Optional:** if you have enough board space, form teams of four or so, each team standing by a section of the board. Within a time limit of about five minutes, each team should write up all the English words they know for non-electronic devices – particularly tools such as **hammer**, and 'kitchen/bathroom/household' words such as **pan** and **toothbrush.**
   Call time and go through the lists, clarifying meaning as necessary. It doesn't matter if the same words appear on different lists.

   Alternatively, if your board is too small, go with the whole class through the alphabet and see how many devices they can think of for each letter – e.g. A- **axe**, B- **bowl, broom**, C- **comb ...** Ask a couple of students to be Secretary and write the words up for you on the board as you work through the alphabet.

2. Tell the class that they are going to be working for a while with words for functional objects called 'devices', a category which includes tools. Add that these words are useful not just because it may be useful to know what to call a particular device but also because they occur in current idioms. Either give one example in English (e.g. **A company may <u>axe</u>** (= suddenly eliminate) **a number of jobs**), or see if you can elicit some mother-tongue device idioms.

3. Form pairs. Give half of the pairs two copies of list A and half two copies of list B.

4. Using mono- or bilingual dictionaries, partners work together to find out what each word means. Ask everybody to convert their word list into a 'mini-dictionary' by either drawing a picture of each device, writing L$_1$ translations or writing

functional descriptions such as 'For sharpening axes and knives'. Students should work in whispers so that the pairs with the other list don't hear their words. Some dictionaries, such as **The Macmillan English Dictionary for Advanced Learners**, provide a great deal of pictorial support as well (Michael Rundell and Gwyneth Fox, eds. 2nd edition, 2007. Macmillan).

5. When everyone understands all the words on their list, ask students to form new pairs. Emphasise that no one should show their list to their partner. Also ask each pair to have ready a sheet of blank paper to draw or write on.

6. In each pair, A and B take it in turns to describe their devices either in terms of parts and materials or in terms of function. (The latter is easier.) As soon as B, for example, thinks he or she knows what device A is describing, B either says the English word, mimes using the device, or draws a picture of it. If B is correct, then it's his or her turn to do the describing. But if B is thinking of the wrong device, A continues giving hints. Finally, if B doesn't know the English word, A tells B and, for instance, shows B a drawing of it.

7. When pairs begin to finish Step 6, call a halt to the exercise and ask partners to show each other their lists and explain to each other the function of any remaining unknown words. Leave review work until the next lesson.

VARIATION

Ask students to review all the target words in preparation for the review and extension, which happens in the next lesson.

REVIEW AND EXTENSION

8. Form students into threes and in each group give one student the Review Sheet. This person quizzes the other two. But ask the quizzers not to work through the questions in the order they are given on the sheet but instead to hop around; this is so that different quizzers won't often be asking the same question at the same time. The Review Sheet includes hints in case any are necessary (see also the Key in the Keys section).

9. As students finish, hand out copies of the Figurative Idioms Sheet.

10. In pairs or threes, students go through the items one by one and see if they can agree about (a) the meaning of the expressions in bold and (b) how the metaphorical meaning might derive from the literal meaning.

11. Bring the class together and check understanding.

12. Do an additional review activity such as 4.4 ('Using chunks in mini-stories').

3.6 Idioms from card playing

> This is another sequence of speaking and thinking activities which focuses on literal meanings as preparation for work on a set of figurative idioms. In this case, the idioms originate from card playing – from poker playing, mostly. We often use these idioms when talking about people who are in some sense in competition with each other (e.g. businesspeople engaged in a negotiation) and who hide or reveal their intentions, have positions of relative advantage, persevere or withdraw and succeed or fail in getting what they want. It doesn't matter if you and/or some of your students are not card players: the materials here should provide all the information you need.

Focus Card-playing idioms such as ***have a showdown***; inferring meanings; intensive reading

Level Upper intermediate +

Time 2 hours over three to four lessons

Materials 6 handouts (see pp.125-129), some of which can be projected rather than photocopied; (a set of Idiom & Meaning slips (Sheet 3) for each pair of students)

Preparation
1. Check out the less technical parts of the Wikipedia entry for poker in order to get an idea about this card game, unless you already know. The key thing is that poker is a very popular game which is usually played for money.
2. **Optional:** on the internet, find an image of Georges de La Tour's painting 'The Card-Sharp with the Ace of Clubs' in colour. (This painting is sometimes also called 'The Cheat with the Ace of Clubs'.) Checking you're not violating copyright laws in your country, prepare to display it (e.g. by means of a colour slide).
3. Prepare your handouts/slides:
   For Sheet 3, make a copy for each pair of students; cut the sheets into jumbled strips (cut the sheet into halves lengthwise, then separate the lines) and put each batch of strips into an envelope.

in class
1. **Optional:** to the whole class, display 'The Card-Sharp with the Ace of Clubs' for a few seconds only, then turn it off and ask the class to tell you what they remember seeing in the picture. Repeat this sequence of showing, turning off and asking before allowing your class a good long look at the painting. Then ask if anyone can tell you something about the painting which they think other people in the class may not have noticed. Finally, if necessary, point out that the man on the left is ***tipping his hand*** (i.e. his hand of cards) so that his opponents can see their values. Ask why he might be doing so. (He probably wants to make the others think he has a poor hand before he dishonestly exchanges one of his weak cards for the ace that he is hiding behind his back. Thus, they will bet more money and he will probably win it.)
2. Find out who plays what card games in your class.

3. Write the following on the board (or project it) and make sure everyone understands it. (The bold type indicates heavy stress.)

> "**P**oker **po**pular? **There's** an understatement. Poker is a con**ta**gion that currently has this country com**plete**ly in its grasp."

From 'The whole world's playing poker', *Daily Telegraph*, UK. 16.6.2005

4. Mention that card playing (especially poker) has been so common for so long in English-speaking countries that it has produced a considerable number of figurative idioms – ones which people are especially likely to use in talk about any kind of negotiation and about interpersonal relations in general.

5. Ask if the students know any mother-tongue idioms that come from card playing.

6. Give out the first sheet, with Handouts 1 and 2 on it, and answer any questions arising.

7. Form pairs (or threes), give each set of students one packet of jumbled idioms and meanings from Handout 3, and allow 10–15 minutes for them to match each idiom with its meaning.

8. To enable students to check, hand out (or display) the Idiom meanings key.

9. Distribute the story (Handout 4). Ask everyone to read the story and then, for each numbered chunk, to:

   a) decide whether it is used in the story literally (L), figuratively (F) or both (L+F), and then

   b) check their judgements with one or more partners.

10. Deal with any queries that arise.

REVIEWING

11. At the end of the lesson, or in the next lesson, hand out the first review sheet (Handout 5) for students to do in pairs or threes.

12. **Optional:** In a still later lesson, hand out the second review sheet (Handout 6), again for students to use in pairs or threes.

3.7 Idioms from seafaring

> This sequence of activities is potentially as much a lesson in culture and history as in language.

Focus Figurative idioms such as *in the wake of*; looking at seafaring, an important aspect of British history and culture; reading, speaking, writing; (optional) reciting a poem

Level Upper intermediate–Advanced, depending on the options adopted

Time Without the optional steps and extension: 40–80 minutes, depending on whether the writing is done in class or as homework.
With all steps: at least two lessons.

Materials Handouts (see pp.130-133)

Preparation **Optional:** Use Google Images ('sailing ships', 'ship's helm', 'pirate', 'pirate ship', 'marina') to find suitable photos. Http://www.mariners-l.co.uk offers a great deal of interesting geographical and historical information (and for nautical terms, see http://www.mariners-l.co.uk/GenBosunSlang.html) . Also, Google 'women pirates'.

in class

1. Write the word *pirate* in the centre of the board and call your class up to the board to produce an instant 'spidergram' or 'mind map'. (To learn about mind maps, see Wikipedia: 'mind map' – http://en.wikipedia.org/wiki/Mind_map) In a large class, ask for two or three volunteers to construct the mind map as you elicit words.

2. When the board is fairly crowded with terms, elicit explanations for any that may not be clear, and see what else your class knows about pirates.

3. Mention that pirates are just one kind of seafarer, and add that now the topic is going to be broadened.

4. In a corner of the board, draw (or ask a student to draw) a quick, *rough* sketch of sailing ship showing (with labels) one or two masts and a couple of sails, the helm (= the 'steering wheel' at the back); some ropes connecting masts with the side of the ship, the bow (= front) of the ship, the keel (the very bottom of the ship) and the wake (= the trail of water behind a moving ship).

   Optional: also display any photo slides you have prepared (ensuring that there are no copyright issues involved in the country you are in).

5. **Optional:** use the four texts in the examples in a jigsaw reading and discussion activity as follows:

   a) Divide the class into three sections and give the students in each section the same text.

   b) The students in a given section read their text and then confer in groups of three about what is interesting and important in their text. They also check that they have the same answers to the questions.

   c) Form new groups of three such that each group of three includes a student who has read a different text.

d) In their new groups, students tell each other what is interesting and important in the text they have read.

One purpose of this step is to give students an idea of why there might be so many sailing idioms in English.

6. Give everyone a copy of the Idiom Sentences sheet, make sure they understand the literal meaning of all the underlined words, and see how many of the idioms they already know, or can guess the meaning of – but don't explain any of them yourself just yet.

7. Dictate the meanings of the idiom sentences as shown here. As you dictate, students should write each meaning by the appropriate idiom. Obviously, as you go along the students will find that this task gets easier (by process of elimination).

Meanings of idiom sentences

It was all plain sailing.	= It was problem-free.
She did it under her own steam.	= without help
I need some leeway.	= freedom and room to manoeuvre
He hasn't been on an even keel since the divorce.	= in (emotional) 'balance'
Everything's shipshape.	= very tidy and in perfect order
Give him a wide berth from now on.	= avoid, don't go near
You'll learn the ropes in your first weeks at work.	= get oriented in a job, learn the basics.
In the wake of a bad earthquake reconstruction is always necessary.	= after (a big event)
Who's going to take the helm after you retire?	= become boss, take control
He just keeled over.	= pass out and fall over
Let's try a different tack.	= a change of direction, a new way of doing something
Don't rock the boat.	= Don't bother people in an organisation by trying to change the way things are done.

---

8. Elicit or announce the correct answers (see the Explanations of Idiom Sentences).

9. For homework, or in class, students each write a very short story (7–9 lines) containing a couple of the seafaring idioms about the first day on the job of an apprentice witch/sorcerer, a novice palaeontologist, or a young pirate. (In the last case, some of the expressions might be used literally rather than as figurative idioms.)

EXTENSION

10. Hand out or display a poem such as 'Sea Fever' (in the examples) and read it out loud to your students, just once. If applicable, mark natural pause points as shown.

11. Give students time to read the poem and ask about vocabulary.

12. Lead choral reading as follows:

a) Everyone reads the poem aloud once in unison.

b) Everyone reads it out again, but the last third of each line is read **silently**. That is, the words before the final slash mark on each line are read out loud, but **the words after the final slash mark are only thought**. NB: the silent part of each line is allotted the same amount of time as if it were actually being spoken.

c) Repeat, but this time everyone reads aloud only the **first** third of each line, always allowing time for the silent reading of the last two-thirds of each line.

d) Everyone reads out the whole poem again.

Acknowledgement
We learned this technique for choral reading of a poem from Peter Grundy.

VARIATION
In Step 5, different students may read texts found on the internet about different pirates, naval commanders, or seafaring explorers (e.g. just Google 'women pirates', 'famous pirates', or 'famous explorers').

3.8 Horse idioms

> This is potentially as much a lesson in culture and history as in language.

Focus   Figurative idioms such as **spur sb on**; speaking; inferring meanings

Level   Intermediate +

Time   45–60 minutes

Materials   A class set of one worksheet (see p. 134); a set of drawings to be displayed/photocopied

Preparation   Prepare to display the horse pictures, or find some in Google Images; (check that there are no copyright issues in the country you are in).

in class

1. With students in groups of three or four, ask one person to talk about a topic which you will assign in a moment. Say that when you call out the topic, the 'talker' in each group must begin talking and that they should try not to stop for 60 seconds (intermediate) or 90 seconds (upper intermediate–advanced). Then announce that the topic is 'horses'.

2. At the end of the time limit, announce that all the groups now have another minute in which anyone in the group can add something about horses.

3. Ask a few people around the class to say something that someone else in their group said about horses. Don't forget to ask if anyone in the class has ridden a horse, has been to a horse-race or has had some other first-hand experience of horses.

4. With the whole class, brainstorm vocabulary connected with horses and write it up on the board under such headings as 'Parts of a horse', 'Equipment', 'Kinds of horses', 'Uses', 'Things horses can do', 'Miscellaneous'.

5. Make sure they know the vocabulary shown in the pictures, and make sure too that they know that in English we don't say horses run; we say they trot, canter and gallop.

6. As to the items of equipment, ask which ones are specifically for controlling a horse in some way. (Those would be, especially, bridles, reins, tethers and spurs.)

7. **Optional:** in a monolingual class, see if anyone knows any L_1 idioms or proverbs which have to do with horses or horse-related equipment.

8. Say that because horses were so important in the past, many English idioms originated from knowledge of horses. Mention that while some of the idioms come from horses being big, strong and sometimes hard to control, other idioms have to do with equipment or with horse racing.

9. Hand out the worksheet. Ask students to go through it either with a partner or individually, as they prefer, and then compare with a partner. Add that they should do two things: first, choose the most likely meaning for each idiom, and then try to agree with their partner about how this meaning might have originated from the literal meaning of (any of) the words in the idiom.

10. Bring the class together and check the idioms one by one.

3.9 Body idioms

> This sequence of vocabulary brainstorming, guessing-from-context and intensive reading activities incorporates techniques you can apply to figurative idioms generally.

Focus Figurative idioms containing body part words, e.g. **toe the line**; inferring meanings; intensive reading. (Variation: listening)

Level Upper intermediate–Advanced, with a variation for Intermediate level.

Time 45–60 minutes

Materials Three handouts (see pp.135-138)

Preparation Make class sets of the handouts.

in class

1. If you have enough board space …
   a) Divide your class into groups and allot each group an area of the board **and** a segment of the alphabet (e.g. a–f, h–m etc).
   b) Ask groups to write onto the board as many 'body part' words they can think of that begin with any of the letters in their assigned portion of the alphabet (e.g. a–f).
   c) After a while, swap the groups around so that each one is facing a list made by another team.
   d) Ask the groups to try to add more words beginning with the relevant letters of the alphabet.
   e) Repeat steps (c) and (d) as appropriate.

   Alternatively, if the board's too small to do that, face the whole class, elicit body-part nouns, and write them up on the board (or ask a couple of 'Secretaries' to do this for you).

2. Form the class into threes or fours. Each group should have a Secretary who notes down what his/her group decides:
   a) what are the typical function(s) of each body part (e.g. cheeks are for putting make-up on and for preventing food from falling out of the sides of our mouths), and
   b) what connotations the noun has (e.g. 'heart': **rather positive**, **romance**, **sensitivity**).

3. Join the groups together into larger groups, and ask the Secretaries to report their group's ideas to the members of the other groups in their new 'mega' group.

4. Hand out the Idioms Sheet and ask students to complete it individually or in pairs, as they prefer.

5. Bring the class together and go through the examples on the Idioms Sheet one by one.
    (**Short key:** the expressions which are **not** figurative are:
    1) **elbow your way**, although it is probably an exaggeration;
    17) **tip-toed**, although there might also be some exaggeration here too; and
    19) which could be seen as being halfway between literal and figurative.)

6. From your class, elicit as much of the story of Little Red Riding Hood as you can. Make sure they know that in the old days, when riding in a cart or on a horse, people used to wear heavy coats (or 'cloaks') which sometimes had hoods on them.

7. Hand out the story of Little Red Riding Hood, and ask students, working individually, to mark each highlighted idiom with an L if it's being used literally, F if it's being used figuratively, and L+F if it could have either sense in this context, or both senses at the same time.
    Ask them also to see if they can spot the idiom which is the odd one out, i.e. an idiom which is highlighted but which **not** a body-part idiom.
    (**Short key:** the odd one out is **couldn't carry a tune in a basket.**
    The full key is shown in the Keys section.)

8. As students finish, ask them to pair up and compare their thoughts.

9. Call the class together and go through the idioms one by one.

10. Ask pairs to (a) join up again as they were, (b) look again at Idioms Sheet 1, and (c) find the idioms which were not used in the story.
    (**Short key:** these are idioms 1–4 & 15 on the sheet of examples).

11. **Optional:** if you are lucky enough to have a large board and if your class is not very large, draw a large figure of a person on the board. Then ask students to come to the board one by one and, from memory, write an idiom near the relevant part of the figure – e.g. to write **give sb the cold shoulder** near a shoulder. Anyone who can't remember an idiom can say "Pass" and remain seated. Students then copy the finished 'idiom map' into their notebooks.

REVIEWING

Option 1:

1. At the beginning of a later class, ask students to form groups of three. In each group, one student draws a large human figure on a sheet of paper. Then, working together, they try to label it with idioms – from memory.

2. When they can't think of any more idioms, they swap sheets with another threesome. Onto the new sheet, they add any idioms that are missing from it.

3. Then they swap back so that they get their original sheet again. They look at any new idioms that have been added by the other trio. Then they check their notebooks to see if they had forgotten any.

Option 2:

1. Hand out the Idioms Review Sheet. Allow students to work through it in pairs if they wish.

2. Then call the class together and go through the items one by one.

3.9 Body idioms

VARIATION (Intermediate +)

Preparation: read through the Idioms Sheet and cross out items you think are not appropriate for your class. Then in the story, cross out the same items, and adjust the text so that it is more natural and simpler than before.

Procedure: instead of Steps 6–10, pre-teach any potentially unfamiliar vocabulary (although there shouldn't be much now that you have simplified it). On the board, write the target chunks in the order they are going to occur in the story, and ask students to copy the list onto a sheet of paper. Say that:

a) you are going to read the story out to them;

b) when you are about to use one of the chunks, you will slow down and point to it on the board; and

c) on their papers, they should mark whether that chunk has been used literally (L), figuratively (F) or both (L+F) (see Step 7 above).

In pairs or threes, students compare their thoughts. Read through the story a second time, more slowly. Whenever you come to a target chunk, stop and make sure everyone understands how it is being used at that point in the story.

3.10

Boxing idioms

This listening and intensive reading activity focuses on a set of idioms, originally from boxing, that are often used to talk about competitions of many kinds.

Focus Figurative idioms such as ***down (*** or ***out) for the count***; (optional) listening & discussion; intensive reading

Level Upper intermediate +

Time 30–45 minutes

Materials **Optional:** 1–3 slides of boxing matches from the internet (check that there are no copyright issues in the country you are in); worksheet (see p.139)

Preparation 1. **Optional:** on the internet, find 1–3 dramatic boxing paintings, e.g. 'Dempsey and Firpo' or 'Stag at Sharkey's' by George Wesley Bellows, or the photo entitled 'First round, First minute Mohammed Ali vs Sonny Liston 25th May 1965' (all of which should be on Google; see also 'boxing' via Google Images). Prepare slides of the images you want to display.
2. Prepare copies of the worksheet.

in class 1. **Optional:** in order to better enable your students to link the boxing idioms with rich mental images, lead a visualisation activity. Ask them to sit comfortably, relax, and close their eyes; when they have sat silently for a few seconds, speak … perhaps as follows (the slashes mark possible dramatic pauses):

You're in a large room. / A very large room. It's called a boxing arena, and in the middle of it is a boxing ring. / It's called a 'ring', but it is in fact square. / There's a post at each corner of the ring. Thick red ropes go from post to post. The function of the ropes is to keep anyone from falling out of the ring. /

The ring is in the centre of this arena and it is raised up a few feet so that if you're in the front row of seats the boxers are a bit above you. / Soon, boxers will fight in this ring. / The ceiling of this arena is high. / There are four entrances to the arena – one on each side; all are higher than the ring. /

The fight is going to start soon. Already there are older men in suits in the ring. Some were famous boxers in the past. Their noses don't look normal; they look squashed. / One by one, they are introduced by another man in a suit. His nose is normal. He is the announcer. / People clap. /

Now tonight's two fighters come into the arena, one after the other. The spectators shout, boo, clap, whistle, stamp their feet, cheer and jeer … you can't hear yourself think! One after the other, the two fighters climb into the ring through the ropes. / The announcer calls out their names as they enter the ring. People continue to cheer and boo./ All the men in suits leave the ring by climbing through the ropes.

Now the referee is in charge. He tells the boxers the rules; for instance, no hitting below the belt (a *low blow*). He tells them how long each round will last. He tells them to fight fair. You hear that there will be ten rounds. The boxers touch gloves, and each goes to his corner, near his assistants, who wait just outside the ring with towels, water and sticking plasters for cuts. /

3.10 Boxing idioms

The referee gives the signal, and the two boxers come out towards the centre of the ring. The cheering and booing stops. You hear thuds as the two men punch and pound each other. The man behind you leans closer to watch. His knees bump the back of your seat. He has whisky on his breath. Lights hang over the ring. The air is thick with the smoke of cigarettes and cigars.

2. **Optional:** display your boxing images. Form groups of three and ask students to:

   a) discuss their reactions to the visualisation (and the images), and

   b) say what their experiences and views of boxing are.

3. See what boxing terms your students know, and write them up on the board.

4. Add the following expressions (in the left-hand column) onto the board, and ask if anyone knows, or is willing to guess, what each one means. Give explanations (right-hand column) as necessary.

be out for the count	If, when knocked down, a boxer does not get onto his feet again before the referee has counted to ten, it's called a 'knockout', and that boxer loses.
lower your guard	A boxer guards his face by holding his gloved fists up in front of his face. Lowering his *guard*, i.e. his fists, makes it easier for his opponent to hit him.
flex your muscles	= show off your upper arm muscles by bending your arm like a *muscle man*. You might do this to intimidate your opponent.
be on the ropes	= be in trouble because your opponent has forced your back against the ropes; and now that you can't move any farther back, he can hit you even more easily.
stick your neck out	= lean your head forward, which can make it easier for your opponent to hit you in the face.
pull a punch	= stop or weaken a punch just before you make contact with your opponent's body. Sometime criminals pay a boxer to lose a fight. In this case, a boxer who has been paid will *pull his punches* so he will not hurt his opponent. On the other hand, he doesn't want the referee or spectators to see that he is not really trying to win.
the gloves are off!	In the very early days of boxing, fighters would sometimes take off their gloves. This increased the possibility that each boxer would injure the other. They might do this if they became really furious with each other.
throw in the towel	A boxer's assistants can signal 'we give up' by throwing one of their towels into the centre of the ring.
be in a tight corner	= be in a difficult spot, like that of a boxer who has been forced into a corner of the ring, where he has reduced freedom of movement.
take it on the chin	= receive a punch on the chin. Sometimes this means 'receive a literal or metaphorical blow, such as a physical punch or harsh criticism, without showing weakness of spirit'.

5. Distribute the worksheet and ask students to complete it.

6. Bring the class together and check and discuss the answers.

Note
For more about using visualisations in the foreign language classroom, see Arnold, Puchta and Rinvolucri (2007).

3.11

What does *it* mean here?

In some idioms the word *it* is a replacement for a word or phrase that used to be there but which – because it was so familiar – was replaced (or is in the process of being replaced) by *it*. For example, the phrase **Shut it!**UK is a shorter (and even ruder!) version of **Shut your mouth!** The following guessing/matching activity is intended to guide students towards a more imagistic, and thus more memorable, understanding of a number of idioms of this sort.

Focus   Idioms with *it* in them; idioms with a missing noun or noun phrase

Level   Intermediate +

Time   40–60 minutes

Materials   Two worksheets (see p.141) to be presented as slides or as handouts

Preparation   1. Adapt the worksheets to focus on idioms suitable for your class.
2. Prepare slides or class sets of handouts.

in class

1. Explain that a number of English idioms, including some considered to be phrasal verbs, become easier to understand, and probably easier to remember if you know what the word *it* originally referred to.

2. Hand out the Idioms and their Meanings sheet, and allow students time to read through it, ask then to ask you for further information about meaning and usage, and complete the task.

   (**Short key:** Swap around the following meanings: 3 & 6, 5 & 8, and 9 & 11.

3. Display/hand out/dictate the list entitled What *it* originally stood for, and ask students to match the lettered items to the numbered idioms on the Meanings sheet.

VARATION
Give learners a smallish selection of alternatives (see also the examples) and ask them to guess what has been dropped from an expression.

3.12 Sorting figurative idioms by source domain

This activity can serve several purposes:
a) Introducing idioms your students may not yet be familiar with.
b) Reviewing / a knowledge of previously learnt idioms.
c) Doing both (a) and (b) in order to create the opportunity for your students to link new input with language and meanings they've already acquired, and to create a positive feedback loop by by enabling students to experience high success rates.

Focus   Figurative idioms deriving from two or three different domains of activity, e.g. transport and entertainment.

Level   Intermediate +

Time   Variable, depending on class size and level, but at least 30 minutes for the main procedure.

Materials   20–40 A4 or A5 sheets, each displaying a figurative idiom (for ideas, see pp.143-144), plus some sticky tape.

Preparation   1. Select a number of figurative idioms that come from *three* different 'source domains' (see 'Idioms Grouped by Source Domain' in the examples). You will need at least one idiom for each pair of students per 'round' (see Step 6 below.).
Make sure you can explain the figurative meaning of each idiom and can also say what its probable origin is. This kind of information can often be found in *The Collins Cobuild Dictionary of Idioms* (2002, 2nd ed.), a corpus-based dictionary which also indicates which idioms are especially common and thus worthy of priority in teaching. Also, good information can generally be found by Googling, e.g., <etymology "beat around (or 'about') the bush">. Such queries are often answered succinctly at: http://www.etymonline.com .

2. Write each idiom you have chosen on an A4 or A5 sheet, large enough to be read by your students if the sheet is stuck to the board.

3. For Step 10, prepare a second set of A4 or A5 sheets with your new choice of idioms. This time, it is a good idea, however, to include in each new round a number of idioms that are guessable on the basis of previously acquired knowledge. For example, if the hunting-based idiom *It's in the bag* has already been dealt with, it may be easy for students to work out the meaning and origin of *a mixed bag*. If the golf-based idiom *(It's) par for the course* has been covered, the idiom *below par* may become guessable too. If *in the driving seat* is understood, then *take a back seat* is likely also to become transparent.

3.12 Sorting figurative idioms by source domain

in class

1. Draw a Venn diagram consisting of three overlapping ovals, as large as possible, on the board and label them, for example:

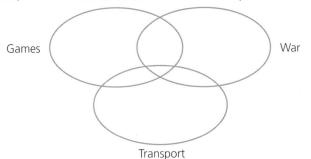

2. Hand out one of the sheets (i.e. one idiom) to each pair of students.

3. Announce that the diagrams represent the three domains of experience that the idioms were originally used in (in their literal sense).

4. Ask each pair:

   a) to explain to their classmates what they think (or remember) the idiom means, and what they think the origin of the idiom is, and

   b) to stick their sheet into the corresponding domain (i.e. oval) on the board. (The overlapping parts of the ovals enable students to place an idiom in two, or even three, source domains at the same time if they think that accurately reflects the idiom's history or if they simply wish to avoid committing themselves to a definite choice.)

5. As sheets are stuck on the board, check the students' ideas about where they should be placed, giving additional information if need be about the origin and/or about the figurative meaning of the relevant idiom. If the choice of source domain was wrong, ask (a member of) the pair to adjust the place of the given idiom in the diagram.

6. Steps 2–5 make one 'round'. For each additional round, you need to give each pair a completely new idiom. (In a class of 16 or so upper intermediate–advanced learners, we do up to five rounds; 40 or so idioms.)

7. After all the sheets are on the board, ask students to work individually (a) choosing an idiom they have **not** presented themselves and (b) inventing a sentence in which they can use the expression figuratively.

8. Ask for volunteers to present their work.

9. Remove all the cards from the board and quiz the students (playfully) about their recollection of some of the expressions and their meanings.

10. Later on in the same session or in a subsequent class, you may wish to 'zoom in' on just one of the (general) source domains in the list in the examples and split it up into more specific ones.
    For example, the domain of 'games' can be split up into (a) card games, (b) horse racing and (c) others. The domain 'sports' can be split up into (a) ball games & track sports, (b) martial arts and (c) shooting contests and hunting. One advantage of such 'zooming-in' is that particular source domains (such

as national sports) that have left a significant mark on the idiom repertoire of a language such as English can be explored more thoroughly, which may help raise students' awareness of the language–culture connection.

At any rate, the procedure is similar to that outlined in Steps 1–8; draw the same kind of partially overlapping diagrams as above and label them according to your choice of particular source domains. Hand out the second set of idiom sheets to pairs of students, and proceed as from 3 above.

EXTENSION

Quite often, the figurative meaning of an idiom is not associated in any obvious way with the original usage of the expression. Although 'etymological' accounts have been proposed, these are not necessarily credible. For example, it has been suggested that the origin of **give someone the cold shoulder** lies in the medieval practice of offering not-so-welcome guests not a hot meal but, instead, the cold leftovers of a piece of meat. Similarly, it has been suggested that the origin of **hear something on the grapevine** lies in the resemblance of early telegraph lines to actual grapevines, and during the US Civil War deceptive telegraph messages sometimes being used by both parties to confuse the enemy.

Instead of relying on these published etymologies, you may wish to stimulate your students' creativity by asking them (e.g. in pairs) to invent an 'etymology' for certain obscure idioms themselves, present their stories in a persuasive way, and vote for the most convincing explanation. Apart from the fun this activity may trigger, it has obvious mnemonic benefits as the students will keep on remembering the idiom around which they have created a story. It is crucial, however, that students first acquire a good understanding of the **figurative** (i.e. idiomatic) meaning of the expressions, so that their etymological stories will truly support idiom comprehension (and not cause confusion instead).

Additional candidate idioms for this activity include: **lead sb up the garden path; sell sb down the river; be alive and kicking; get sb's goat; it's raining cats and dogs,** and **teach your granny to suck eggs.**

REVIEWING

Because of their figurative nature, most of the idioms recommended for sorting by source domain lend themselves well to pictorial/visual illustration. For example, **in the wake of s'thing** can be depicted by drawing a boat with waves behind it, and g**etting into gear** can be mimed by manipulating an imaginary gear stick. As review/consolidation, ask students either to make a drawing on the board or to perform a mime that hints at a particular idiom that they have in mind, so that their peers can guess what it is. The basic procedure here is as follows.

1. Give students a couple of minutes (a) to list for themselves a number of idioms they remember from the previous activities and (b) to select from their list a couple of idioms whose literal meaning they can elucidate either in a drawing or through mime.

2. Ask volunteers to take turns at either drawing on the board or miming their

idiom so as to enable their classmates to guess which one the presenter has in mind.

VARIATION

1. Give each student two or more cards, each with a previously encountered idiom on it, and tell everyone to keep their cards to themselves. (The rationale for giving each student at least two cards is to increase the chances that everyone will be able to perform the next step.)

2. Ask students each to choose an idiom, then tell their fellow-students, "You're looking for an expression that means (…)," and make a drawing on the board that will help classmates identify the expression.

As another alternative, two teams can take turns trying to identify the idiom being drawn or mimed by a member of their own team. (This game-like activity is often known as 'Pictionary'.)

3.13

Talking about an emotion

This suite of activities focuses directly on figurative idioms used in talking about anger. More generally, it invites students to consider the imagery of individual idioms in terms of broad conceptual metaphors (e.g. **anger is a hot liquid**). Doing this can help your students to remember the idioms; it can also play a part in making them better able to interpret unfamiliar figurative idioms that they might meet in the future.

Focus Figurative idioms having to do with anger

Level Upper intermediate +

Time 30–40 minutes

Materials A class set of the handout on p.144, or a slide; in an advanced class, this material can be dictated

Preparation Prepare to hand out or display the text.

in class

1. Ask students to list things that happen to people when they get very angry – e.g. they may get red in the face, become irrational, raise their voice and even become violent.

2. Ask students to read the first text and underline all the figurative phrases that are used to describe an emotion.

3. Bring the class together and ask:

    a) what is it that most of the expressions have in common? (**Short key**: anger is described as if it were a hot gas or liquid inside the body.)

    b) which of the physical symptoms of anger brainstormed in Step 1 seems to have inspired most of the imagery that is expressed?
    (**Short key**: angry people get red in the face and/or seem hot owing to a sudden increase of blood flow to the surface of the body, the head in particular.)

4. Remind students of the other two things that may happen to people when they get very angry: they become irrational and aggressive.

5. Hand out (or dictate or display) the list of Figurative Expressions of Anger and ask students, in pairs, to decide whether the imagery of each of the expressions has to do with heat, madness or dangerous animals.

6. Bring the class together and elicit idioms in your students' mother tongue(s) which express images similar or identical to those expressed by the English idioms considered above. This is most straightforward when students all speak the same L₁ but is also possible in multi-lingual classes.

Tip
For lists of idioms in sets (e.g. TIME IS MONEY: **spend time, buy time, have time to spare...**) see http://cogsci.berkeley.edu/lakoff/metaphors/.

3.14 Seeing the deep logic of word partnerships

This activity helps students to see how the partnerships of a word like **perform** e.g. **perform a song, perform a trick, perform a miracle** – reflect a deep logic. Students who see this logic should find all these phrases easier to remember. Here, we focus on a small set of verbs, but the method used is easy to use with other words and other parts of speech.

Focus Verb + noun collocations of *commit, conduct, perform, cause*; (optional: *wreak, carry, improvement* and *progress*)

Level Intermediate–Upper intermediate; also Advanced if you do the extensions

Time 20–30 minutes without the extensions

Materials A class set of the worksheet (see p.145), or 4 picture slides

Preparation Prepare a class set of the worksheet (in the examples) or a slide of each of the pictures (see also 5.28).

in class

1. Write the following verbs on the board with a lot of room beneath each one: **commit, conduct, perform, cause**. As a hint about **conduct**, make sure your students know that a 'conductor' is the leader of an orchestra who tells musicians what, how and when to play. Regarding **perform**, make sure they know that a performance takes place in front of spectators or an audience.

2. Ask students to suggest direct objects for each verb – e.g. for **commit** they may suggest **a crime.** Write each appropriate noun on the board under the verb it typically follows.

3. Ask your students if they can see any general pattern in the kind of direct object that follows each verb.

4. **Option 1:**
   Hand out the worksheet and ask your students to write each of the nouns (e.g. **adultery**) under the appropriate verb (e.g. **commit**). Some of these nouns they should already have mentioned in Step 2.

   Option 2:
   a) Ask your students to write the four verbs (**commit**, etc) on a blank sheet of paper with plenty of room around each one.
   b) Display the four pictures (above) and ask which goes with **commit**, which with **investigate**, etc.
   c) Dictate the nouns (e.g. **adultery**); students should write each one under/ beside the appropriate verb – e.g. **COMMIT: adultery, a crime ...**

5. Check how they did.

6. Check the students' appreciation of how some of the more peripheral cases fit the overall pattern. In particular, ask them why **suicide** goes with **commit** (i.e. it used to be punishable as a crime!) and why **miracle** goes with **perform** (i.e. witnesses – an audience – are generally required).

EXTENSIONS

7. The main procedure focuses on the usual types of direct objects for each of the four target verbs. For example, in the case of *cause*, the aim (by working with such very negative-result nouns as *devastation*) was to highlight its strong link with negative results.

   So now, as an extension, dictate other nouns/phrases and ask students to group them according to how likely they might be to follow *cause*: e.g. **problems, trouble, an improvement, us some difficulty, pain, pleasure, a delay, extra efficiency, disruption …**

8. Introduce your students to the Collins free on-line concordance and collocations sampler at http://www.collins.co.uk, and then ask them to call up concordance lines and the collocations list for:

   a) *commit*, *conduct*, *perform* and *cause*, in order to learn more about their word partnerships;

   b) *investigation* and *inspection*, which should lead them to find that the verb *carry out* is a common alternative to *conduct*;

   c) positive nouns such as *improvement* and *progress*, in order to find out what verbs typically precede them; and/or

   d) the verb *wreak* (past: *wreaked*) used in speaking of extreme forms of damage), which will lead them to the chunk **wreak havoc**.

Note

Both *conduct* and *perform* can partner *operation*. The reason surgeons are said to 'perform' operations (which take place in an **operating theatre**) is that until recent times, it was quite common for there to be spectators! 'Conduct' is used to refer to military and clean-up operations which, like investigations, should involve great attention to detail.

3.15

Stop to smoke? Stop smoking?

Although many course books and grammar exercise books cover the thorny topic of verb complementation with **to** or **-ing**, the explanations given (if any!) generally ignore the fact that **to** retains the essence of its normal prepositional meaning, i.e. **to town** = ➡ town .

The aim of this activity is to leave students with the feeling that this aspect of English is **not** random and chaotic, and that it is worthwhile noticing and reflecting on form and meaning an essential first step to durable learning. This creates an essential first step to durable learning of which combination of forms is appropriate for what context.

Focus   Verb + verb combinations with **to** and **-ing**

Level   Intermediate +

Time   30–45 minutes, not counting the extension

Materials   Class sets of the handout on p.146, or a slide
For the extension, a course book or grammar exercise book containing a set of exercises that can be adapted for this activity

Preparation   Prepare to hand out or display the exercise given in the examples.

in class

1. Remind your class of the following:
   a) If you go 'from A to B', e.g. from school to home, first you are at your starting point and then you are at your destination, like this: = 1 ➡ 2
   b) A sentence like **I want to see that film** has exactly the same semantic structure.
      First comes the 'wanting', and then comes the 'seeing the film', like this: 1 want ➡ 2 see The word **to** has the same meaning in (b) as in (a), i.e. ➡ 2 .

2. Talk your class through three more examples, perhaps as follows:
   a) If I plan to visit someone, which comes first – the plan or the visit?
      Of course the plan comes first. The visit is the 'goal', which is like a destination except it is an action, not a place.
   b) If I remember to buy milk, which comes first?
      The remembering, of course.
   c) If I fail to win the lottery, which comes first?
      The failing! Winning the lottery didn't happen of course – but, like buying the milk, it was still the goal.

   In short, the verb + to-verb structure means that the ideas and actions are **not** in reverse time order. Often, the second verb represents some kind of goal.

3. Give out/display the list of sentences in the handout, and ask students to find and mark the verb + verb combinations which are **not** in time order and in which the second verb does **not** clearly represent a goal.

4. Stress, again, that the verb-to-verb pattern is similar in meaning to the place-to-place structure.
   Then write the following two sentences on the board and ask if the students can work out which, if any, comes first – the starting or the attending:

   I've started attending dancing classes.
   I've started to attend dancing classes.

   In this case, the starting and attending actually happen at the same time, and this is why both the **to** and the **-ing** forms are possible.

5. Write up these two sentences and ask, "In which sentence does **tell/telling** represent a goal?":
   I <u>tried</u> to <u>tell</u> her a joke, but I couldn't remember the end.
   I <u>tried</u> <u>telling</u> her a joke, but even that didn't make her smile.

   In the first, telling the joke is the goal even though it wasn't achieved. In the second, telling a joke was a (failing) means to the goal of making someone smile, but telling the joke was not itself the goal.

6. Write up **I like swimming here** and **I like to swim here**, and explain that for many people, especially speakers of North American English, these sentences differ slightly in meaning in a way that is consistent with the other examples above. That is, **I like to swim here** is something you might say when you are not swimming but are merely thinking of swimming as a desirable goal. But **I like swimming** is something you are especially likely to say when you are actually swimming or when you are picturing yourself in the water having a good time; that is, the (idea of) swimming comes before the (idea of) liking. Add, however, that the difference is very subtle, and absent in British English where **I like -ing** is the norm for both senses.

EXTENSION
Find an appropriate set of exercises from a course book or grammar exercise book for your students to do according to the explanations given above.

3.16 Noticing patterns of sound repetition

> This exercise, which finishes with writing and reading out dialogues, encourages students to notice mnemonic patterns of sound repetition such as alliteration. This reflects experimental evidence that, by directing students' attention to sound repetitions even for a short time, you can increase the chances that students will remember the chunks in question (see p.19).

Focus Any kind of chunk which showings sound repetition (e.g. alliteration); dialogue writing

Level Pre-intermediate +

Time 45–70 minutes, but Steps 1–6 and 7–12 can be done in separate lessons

Materials A list of alliterative film titles; copies of the Which is Catchiest? worksheets (see pp.147-151)

Preparation
1. Steps 1–7: Find a collection of English film titles (e.g. by Googling 'film titles') and select a number of titles that are alliterative (e.g. **Bedknobs and Broomsticks**; **Bend it like Beckham**; **Baby Boom**; **Bullets over Broadway**, **Beauty and the Beast, Dancer in the Dark, Die Another Day, Dirty Dancing, Doctor Doolittle, Mad Max, Desperately Seeking Susan**).
You will not have to look hard, since the use of catchy sound patterns is a common marketing gimmick in the entertainment business (e.g. **Donald Duck, Mickey Mouse, Marilyn Monroe**).
2. Steps 7–12: Prepare a 'Which is the Catchiest?' worksheet by choosing one of the lists in the examples and adding to it or shortening it as appropriate – about 10 items at pre-intermediate level, 15–20 at advanced level.

in class
1. Present students with your list of film titles and ask what they have in common.
2. Invite some discussion about the reason why (English) movie titles often show repetition of word-initial consonants.
3. Elicit examples of the same phenomenon in TV series (**Big Brother, The Bold and the Beautiful**), advertising (**Guinness is good for you**), propaganda (**Back to basics**), and literature (e.g. **Pride and Prejudice, Sense and Sensibility**).
4. Ask students (in groups) to make a brief list of the titles of films they have seen in the past few years and then mark any that show a similar catchy sound pattern.
5. Ask students to contemplate the titles that do not display any catchy sound patterns and invite them to invent alternative titles that do feature repetition of word-initial consonants (i.e. alliteration).
6. Invite students to explain the link between their catchy title and the contents/ nature of the film.
7. Distribute copies of one of the 'Which is catchiest?' worksheets, and ask students to follow the instructions given at the top.

8. Call the class together. Go through the items one by one, leading brisk choral repetition of each 'catchiest' chunk. (The full scope of each chunk is indicated by italics.)

9. Ask each person now to choose 5–8 chunks that they would particularly like to remember, and write them on a sheet of paper.

10. Ask everyone to team up with a partner and exchange papers. Each partner in a pair now dictates the other person's phrases back to them. (It particularly helps memory formation to hear and to write down such phrases.)

11. Ask everyone now to work with a partner to try script a dialogue, one per pair, using some of the expressions that were dictated. Write some possible participants and topics on the board (but tell them they can also invent one of their own): *Two friends talking about someone they (don't) like, Two friends in a shop, Two angels deciding whether a certain celebrity should be allowed into heaven, A couple trying to make a big decision, Two people praising one person and criticising another, Two people discussing some event that they both lived through.*
    As an extra writing prompt, suggest also the first words that the first person says, e.g. "Did you notice …?"

12. As pairs finish, they join up with others and read out their dialogues. The ideal group size is eight.

QUIZZING

Create quiz items by taking the original sentences in the worksheets (in the examples) and deleting all but the initial of each target word, like this:

We had **a whole** | **h_____ / crowd** | of problems.

or all but the 'lead', like this:

We had **a whole** | **ho_____ / crowd** | of problems.

3.17

Sorting by sound

> This suite of activities begins with a 'taster', an awareness-raising activity that focuses on alliteration. Then come additional activities designed to raise learners' awareness of the other patterns of sound repetition discussed in Chapter 1.10.

Focus Any kind of chunk which shows sound repetition, e.g. rhyme

Level Pre-intermediate +

Time 20–40 minutes

Materials **Optional:** a handout showing the phrases to be sorted (for example, see pp.152-153)

Preparation
1. We have suggested that as you progress through a course you keep a record of chunks that have come up which show patterns of sound repetition. Now's the time to use them!
2. Choose 15 or more of those chunks – showing different kinds of patterning – that you want your students to review, and then add in five or so other chunks that show no sound repetition at all.
3. Prepare a jumbled list (such as the one in the examples) for display or for distribution on a handout.

in class
1. Make sure your students are familiar with all of the patterns of repetition that are represented in your list of chunks.

2. Display or hand out the list of expressions, and check that everyone remembers what the chunks mean.

3. Ask your students to sort the underlined chunks into groups according to type of repetition of sound. Suggest they do this by writing the chunks in groups on a separate sheet of paper under the headings Alliteration, Assonance, Consonance, Rhyme, Word repetition, None of these. Tell them that some of the chunks will go under two headings, and a few under three. Allow them to work individually or in pairs, as they prefer.

4. As students finish, ask individuals to pair up, and those already in pairs to find new partners. In these new pairs, students compare their groupings of the chunks.

5. Call the class together and check the group-membership of the expressions, one by one.

6. **Optional:** near the end of the lesson, ask students not to look at their notes. Then, on the board, write the headings 'Rhyme', 'Assonance', 'Alliteration', and 'Other Consonant Repetition'.
In a small class, ask everyone to come to the board and see how many of the target chunks they can write (from memory) under the appropriate heading for each. In a large class, elicit chunks orally while one or two volunteers write the chunks on the board.

CHAPTER 4
REVIEWING AND QUIZZING

Introduction

Although it is well known that periodic review greatly improves students' long-term recall of targeted vocabulary, published materials for chunk teaching tend to give insufficient guidance about how to review chunks.

The aim of this chapter is to go some way towards remedying this deficiency. All the review procedures described here can be used again and again to review different sets of chunks. Each procedure has been designed to achieve most or all of the following aims:

- To encourage students to **re**-notice particular chunks, an essential step if memories are to be at all significantly strengthened.

- To build in the high levels of learner involvement known to be important in memory formation.

- To consolidate, or even extend, understanding of the chunks by presenting them in a context, possibly a new one.

- To require effortful recall, which is known to help vocabulary stick in long-term memory.

- To produce the kinds of deep or elaborative[G] mental processing known to help promote memorisation. This involves encouraging students to associate target chunks with images and with what they already know about English vocabulary and culture.

- To require students to hear, say and write chunks, not just read them.

- To encourage students to guess meanings on the basis of hints which make it likely that guessing will usually be successful (which is personally motivating).

To make reviewing easier to stage, keep a record of those chunks you have targeted as being especially worth learning. But you also need to think about which of those chunks merit extra attention. One criterion here is frequency. Luckily, idiom and phrasal verb dictionaries now generally give guidance about how frequently used any particular idiom or phrasal verb is. Frequency, however, is only part of what you need to consider: another important criterion in deciding which chunks to spend time on is whether a chunk is likely to be **memorable** – e.g. Does it show a sound repetition such as alliteration? Can students be helped to see an underlying metaphor? Is there a similar chunk in your students' mother tongue? Does the chunk key in with an interest that they are likely to have?

Finally, don't forget to try out the reviewing and quizzing exercises described at the end of some of the activities in Chapters 2 and 3.

4.1

Memory slips with hints

> The aim of this relatively short recall exercise, which demands concentration and effort, is to help students remember the exact wording of the chunks targeted. It works best in classes of fewer than 20 students.

Focus Almost any kind of chunk

Level Intermediate +

Time 5–20 minutes

Materials Sets of cut up idiom slips (see p.155)
Optional: a class set of an explanations handout (see p.154)

Preparation
1. Choose a set of 8–15 phrases you want to review. Make sure they don't share any key words; for instance, avoid targeting **high hopes** and **pin your hopes on** at the same time.

2. **Optional:** make an Idiom Explanations Sheet like the one shown in the examples, either for distribution as handouts, or for projection.

3. Make slips like those shown in the examples. You'll need a complete set for each pair of students in your class.

in class
1. Check that students can recall the meanings of the phrases you have decided to target.

2. Display or distribute the Idiom Explanations Sheet, and give students time to look it over.

3. Remove (or ask students to put away) the explanations sheet and form pairs (A & B).

4. Give each pair a complete set of slips, and ask them to spread their slips out in front of them, all turned face down.

5. Tell everyone they are going to do a memory exercise, as follows:

   a) Student A turns over a slip. There is the initial letter of a word on it; if A can remember the word, A can take the slip and keep it. Otherwise, the slip must be replaced and turned face down again.

   b) Regardless of whether A has been able to claim a slip or not, B takes her/his turn to repeat step (a).

   c) Partners alternate until all the slips have been claimed.

6. As pairs finish, form them into groups of four, and collect their slips.

7. In each group of four, one student, looking at the explanations sheet, quizzes the other three by calling out a key word from each idiom. For instance, she or he calls out 'Sleeve', and someone else from the group should call out **Wear your heart on your sleeve**.

4.2 Literal? Figurative? Either? Both?

> In this intensive reading, elaborative processing[G] activity, students work with one or more specially made texts which include idioms they have met before that can, depending on context, have either a literal or a figurative meaning, or both.

Focus Chunks which can have either a literal or a figurative meaning

Level Intermediate +

Time 15–20 minutes

Materials A class set of handouts (or a projectable display) of a story

Preparation
1. Choose a dozen or more idioms that you want to review, and work them into one or more texts, sometimes using them figuratively/idiomatically, sometimes literally, or sometimes ambiguously, between the two. Like this:

   a) *At morning inspection, all soldiers must stand at inspection with the toes of their shoes touching the same imaginary line. Now and then, if the line isn't straight, you might hear an officer say, "Toe the line, soldier!"* (Literal)

   b) *"Look, if you want to keep working for this company, you'd better toe the line. So don't come in late again."* (Figurative)

   c) *In the armed forces, people who refuse to toe the line may find themselves in constant trouble.* (Most likely figurative but conceivably also literal)

2. More ambitiously, you could invent a single, longer narrative or start with a text you find in a newspaper or on the internet, and insert your chunks into it. For instance, you might work the expressions into a version of 'Little Red Riding Hood' (see the examples) or some other traditional tale. The essential thing is to use some of the expressions literally and some figuratively.

3. Prepare projection slides or a class set of photocopies of your text(s).

in class
1. Explain the task and give everyone a handout. For each underlined chunk, students should indicate whether it is used literally or figuratively or both, by labelling it L, F, or L+F.

2. As students finish, they each compare their labelling with that of a partner.

3. With the whole class, quickly check answers and sort out any problems. Note also that it is perfectly legitimate, in some contexts, for some readers to see an expression as literal but for others to see it as figurative.

4.3 Circulating review sheets

The main purpose of this versatile exercise is to help students remember the full written form of chunks which fall into families (e.g. weather expressions, phrasal verbs, proverbs). In the case of 'topic linked' chunks (weather expressions, expressions relating to horses, etc.) this activity should help students form durable mental associations between each chunk and a topic area, something which should facilitate long-term recall of the chunks themselves.

Focus   Any kind of chunk

Level   Pre-intermediate +

Time   15–25 minutes

Materials Blank sheets of paper

Preparation Think of three families of chunks you have targeted recently and which you want your students to review – e.g. similes (**as blind as a bat)**, situational expressions (**Small world!**), and idioms stemming from a domain of activity such as sailing (**jump ship**).

in class

1. Ask students to pair up, with one full-size blank sheet of paper per pair.

2. Following a clear route through the room (e.g. start with the pair left-front and finish with the pair in the right-rear of the room) call the first pair A, the second B, the third C, then the fourth A, the fifth B and so on.

3. Tell your students that soon they will be passing papers along your route. (You may need to help pass papers from the last to the first pair on your route.)

4. Announce that all the A pairs will be in charge of (for example) similes, all the Bs will be in charge of situational clichés, and all the Cs will be in charge of sailing idioms. Explain that the 'simile' pairs should head their paper 'Similes' and **from memory** list on it as many as possible of the similes that have been encountered in class so far. Tell the other pairs they should do the same with whatever type of chunk you have given them.

5. Begin the activity. When some pairs have stopped writing, call time and say that each pair should:

   a) pass their sheet to the next pair along the route

   b) then try to add to the list that they have just received from the pair up the line; for instance, an A pair which started with similes will now have a list of sailing idioms (from a C pair) which they should try to extend.

6. Ask pairs to team up with one or two other pairs that started with the same kind of chunk. They sit or stand together and compare their lists.

4.4

Using chunks in mini-stories

> Various methodologists have recommended that students be encouraged to write highly codified text types such as the limerick, the haiku and the mini-saga. However, for reviewing chunks, we have found it best to ask students to write within a more flexible framework, that of the super-short story.

Focus Any kind of chunk; creative writing; reading aloud

Level Pre-intermediate +

Time 20–25 minutes

Materials Blank sheets of paper

Preparation
1. Choose a set of chunks to focus on – e.g. idioms from card playing, phrasal verbs met this week, chunks from the dictation you did recently. So when they come to hear or read each other's stories, the same few chunks are likely to come up again and again, which should fix them more firmly in the students' minds

2. Decide on a cast of characters. The 'three character' story described below is very versatile. However, for some sets of chunks other types of story may work better. For example, we have found that seafaring idioms go well with the task of describing a young sorcerer's (witch's / wizard's / palaeontologist's / ghostbuster's) first day on the job, perhaps because of the meanings of expressions such as **learn the ropes** and **try a new tack**.

in class
1. List three characters (e.g. Princess + Pirate + Parrot; or Archaeologist + Desert bandit + Camel; or Magician + Prince(ss) + Frog; or Private detective + (jealous) Wife/Girlfriend + (jealous) Husband/Boyfriend) on the board, and explain that the task is to write a 7–9 sentence story which includes (a) at least two of the characters plus (b) two or three chunks from the set you decided on in Preparation 1.

2. **Option 1:**
Ask students to write the stories in class. As students finish, ask them to stand or sit with others who have finished, and read each other their stories silently, or take turns reading them to each other out loud. (This solves the problem of what to do with early finishers.) Then collect the stories for later editing by you.

Option 2:
Set the writing for homework and collect it in a later lesson. When you have edited the stories, hand them back for students to read to each other in groups of five or so.

Tip
Allow students to write about other characters, and to write more than your upper limit of nine sentences if they like. Don't use up all your good ideas for characters at once by giving your class choices of different sets of characters. It's better if you can keep some characters in reserve for reviewing other sets of chunks.

4.5 What comes next?

This intensive reading and reading-aloud exercise is extremely versatile, and is designed to review the phrasing of any particular text students have previously worked with – a text in their coursebook, for example. You might be surprised how much your students enjoy doing it. You may, though, need to precede this activity with some work on reading aloud (see Activity 2.1).

Focus   Any kind of chunk

Level   Upper elementary +

Time   5–20 minutes, depending on the text

Materials   Class sets of text handouts (se Preparation)

Preparation
1. *Use a text that your students have already encountered* – perhaps earlier in the same lesson. It can range from several, to several dozen, sentences long.

2. Divide a long text into sections, one per student. Insert slashes immediately before words which the students should be able to recollect, or at least guess, from what they have met before, like this:

> An amateur sailor endured 24 hours in the cold North // Atlantic after being swept // off his one-man sailing boat by towering // waves. Searchers had given up // hope for the man, who was barely // alive when he was found on a beach in Norway by a dog // walker. When interviewed later he said, "I nearly froze to // death. People told me the weather was too bad to sail in. I wish I had listened // to them!"

in class
1. Form pairs, trios or foursomes. In each pair or group, one student (A) should have the original text.

2. Student A reads the text out, but with pauses at the slash marks. When A pauses, her/his partner(s) should guess the next word or the rest of the phrase. Student A should give hints as necessary, for example by giving the first sound or letter of the word that should come next or through use of gesture or mime.

3. When A has finished reading her/his (part of) the text, B takes over.

Tips

It is important that you demonstrate how to give hints by using gesture or mime – e.g. in order to elicit the last word of a dog walker you can move your fingers in a way that suggests walking.

If you need to reduce noise, have students working in groups of three or four rather than in pairs. Again, assign each student a different (part of) a text to read out.

If everyone is using the same text at the same time, they can be distracted by what they hear other groups say. So it is a good idea to review two or three different texts at the same time, but giving the texts in different order to groups near one another. So each group works with all the texts, but in different orders.

4.6

Review posters

All the options described here involve using abbreviations to prompt the recall of chunks you want to review.

Focus Any kind of chunk

Level Any

Time **Option 1:** 5–10 minutes
Option 2: 10–15 minutes, for a class of 20

Materials Broad nib felt-tip markers; for Option 1, a couple of sheets of full size poster paper with a stock of more held in reserve; for Option 2, sheets of ordinary size paper.

Option 1:
Wall posters for chunks BEING LEARNED and PRETTY WELL LEARNED

Preparation Put up two large wall posters; let's call them A (for Being Learned) and B (for Pretty Well Learned). Poster A will be for the initials of chunks which most people in the class understand but are unable to recall even when prompted by a translation or a clue about its meaning or how it works. Poster B will be for chunks which started out on poster A but which almost everyone can finally recall when they are given a clue.

in class
1. When you notice that your students are not remembering a target chunk, write its initials on poster A. But be flexible about what constitutes an initial; for prompts to be helpful, they need to indicate the **sounds** the words start with, so 'wr. h.' is a much better hint for **wreak havoc** than is 'w. h.'.

2. At least once a lesson, use the initials which have accumulated on poster A to cue recall of the full chunks. A simple way of doing this would be to point to a set of initials – e.g. **N. m.** (for **Never mind.**) – and say, "We may say this to mean 'Forget what I said; it's not important'. What's the phrase?" Or ask, "What's this phrase, and when do we say it?"

3. When most of your students can remember a chunk represented by initials on poster A, cross the initials out and write them on poster B. Review the chunks on poster B perhaps once a week.

4. When either poster is full, cover it with a blank one.

5. Now and then review the chunks on any old Pretty Well Learned posters that have been covered up by new ones.

QUIZZING

For each set of initials on poster B, give a gapped context. Students have to fill in the gaps by expanding initials (which they can see on the poster) into fully worded phrases.

Option 2:
Small posters

Preparation

To create a bit more interest and encourage personal investment, put individual students in charge of one or more posters, on normal sized sheets of paper, which they keep in their files/ring binders. Each sheet shows the initials of just one phrase, in large, bold writing so that students on the other side of the room can read them.

in class

1. Once in a while, ask everyone to take out one of their posters, stand around the walls facing each other, and hold their poster up so that others can see it.

2. Ask everyone around the room to read out the chunk represented by the initials on their poster. This is an opportunity for them to ask about any phrase whose meaning or wording they can't remember.

3. Ask students to stand in pairs.

4. Call on one pair of students and ask them to point to (any) three posters they can see and say the whole phrase for each.

5. Ask another pair to point to four posters and say the whole phrase for each.

6. Repeat a few more times, each time setting a higher number of posters.

7. Ask each pair to make sure they know the phrases of the pair standing to their left.

8. Working around the circle, ask each pair to call out the phrases of the pair on their left.

9. Ask a few students to move to a different place in the circle.

10. Ask everyone to find their old partner again and, all at once, to look around at all the posters and see how many they can both remember.

Tip

One way to help students remember the form and meaning of their own phrase is to ask them to add onto each Initials poster a sketch which hints at the meaning of the phrase, and/or to write a translation on the back, in very small letters.

4.7

Guess my chunk

> This activity is a game-like way of reviewing one or two chunks, to be done at the beginning or end of a lesson.

Focus   Idioms

Level   Pre-intermediate +

Time   5–15 minutes

Materials   For the second variation: a supply of paper for slips

Preparation   None

in class

1. Explain that you will all be playing a version of the well known game Twenty Questions. One volunteer student will think of and secretly write down an idiom. Then others in the class ask Yes/No questions such as: *Does it have more than five words?, Does the first word have three letters or fewer?, Is the middle word a preposition?, Did you learn it this week?, Was it in a story?, Does it come from an activity in this course?, Has it come from seafaring?, Does it have to do with being able to feel things?, Does it alliterate?, Is it positive?* If by the time the volunteer has answered 20 questions nobody has guessed the idiom, then the volunteer has won.

2. Call volunteers to the front of the class one by one.

VARIATIONS

- Divide the class into groups of four or so. Group members take turns answering questions about their own personal chunk.

- With your back to the board:

   1. Ask everyone to write an idiom and their name on a small slip of paper; collect these slips.

   2. Ask one student, the 'guesser', to stand at the front of the class a couple of metres from the board and facing away from it. Ask the guesser not to turn around and look at the board.

   3. Choose one of the idioms on the slips (but not the guesser's own idiom) and write it on the board behind the guesser so that he or she cannot see it.

   4. The guesser now asks questions such as the ones listed above. This may work best if the guesser calls on particular parts of the class, e.g., "Anyone sitting by the door – does it have more than five words?", "Anyone in the back row – does it come from the world of horses?"

4.7 Guess my chunk

- Charades/Pictionary: One by one, volunteers come to the board, each with an idiom in mind. By means of gesture, mime and drawing, they try to help the class guess the idiom they are thinking of.

- Guess the Initials:

  1. Ask everyone to look through their notes and find a chunk which they think others in the class ought to remember.

  2. As students think of chunks, they come to the board (not necessarily one by one) and write just the beginnings of each word in the chunk. For instance, **Don't hold your breath!** might be written up like this: **Do__ h___ y___ br____!**

  3. When the board is covered with clues, point to the initials one by one, and see if anyone other than the person who wrote it up can guess what they stand for.

4.8 Test me easy, test me hard

The basic idea here is that students can choose before a quiz whether to be tested 'easy' or 'hard'. For example, if you had a text in both full and in gapped versions, you could let students choose whether to try to fill in the gapped text before reading the full version (the hard way) or whether to read the full text before trying to fill in the gaps (the easy way). Here, we describe how students can quiz each other about chunks which can occur at, or near, the end of a sentence. One element of the rationale for this particular exercise is that memories of chunks are best entrenched when students not only read target language but hear and say it too.

Focus   Chunks that can come at/near the end of a sentence

Level   Pre-intermediate +

Time   10 minutes

Materials   One handout for each student (for examples, see p.156)

Preparation
1. Choose 8–10 chunks to review.
2. For each chunk, write a number of short passages (single sentences mostly) like those in the example worksheets. That is, in each short context the target chunk should come at or near the end; also each context should suggest the meaning of the chunk which it contains. To help students remember them, make sure that the chunks are not too similar in either in form or meaning – e.g. do not target both ***come into (an inheritance)*** and ***come by (a new possession)*** simultaneously.

in class
1. Distribute the handout, and give students time to read it and ask questions about the meaning of any of the chunks.
2. Ask everyone to turn over their sheet, and then test them as follows. Read out each item, but always stop at the ***last*** double slash; this is the easy test. Anyone in the class who remembers the end of the item should call it out.
3. Ask students to pair up and, reading from the handout, take turns testing each other in the same way you tested the class. The student being tested can say, "Test me easy!" (= pause at the last double slash), "Test me medium!" (= pause at the middle double slash, if there is one), or "Test me hard!" (= pause at the first).
4. Ask students to turn their papers face down again, and then work in pairs to try to write as many of the sentences as they can.

4.9 Spoken team quizzes

> This is a fun quiz and listening activity that can provide very useful review and also give you a pretty good idea about who has remembered what, even though it does not yield individual scores.

Focus   Any kind of chunk, except grammatical ones such as *as ... as ...*

Level   Beginner +

Time   10–30 minutes

Materials   None

Preparation   Jot down a Chunk Quiz which you can deliver orally. We have provided some examples of different types of question (see p.157).

in class

1. Ask students to pair up for a Team Quiz.
2. Explain that:
   a) each team needs **one** answer sheet, and that only one team member (the 'secretary') should write on it, and
   b) when you call out a quiz item, team members can confer, but **only** in very quiet whispers.
3. Ask the secretaries to write numbers down the sides of their papers according to the number of quiz items there are going to be, and then call out an example quiz item to see how well students have understood what to do.
4. Read out your test items.
5. Correct the quiz orally by talking through the items. Ask the secretaries to change to a pen or pencil of different colour when correcting their papers, or ask teams to swap and then correct each other's sheets, or just treat the quiz as a learning experience pure and simple, and let each team correct their quiz sheets as they like.
6. Collect papers, or ask different pairs how they did (e.g. "Who got a stupendous score?", "Who only got a wonderful one?", "Whose score was pretty good?", "So so?", "Utterly disastrous – we don't know what happened!").

4.10

Embedding chunks in a text

In this exercise students decide how a small set of chunks can be inserted into a text. For each chunk, this challenges students to consider:
- its functional class, e.g. adjective
- what it does, e.g. describe a noun
- its meaning.

Focus Any kind of chunk, except grammatical chunks like *as ... as...*

Level Elementary +

Time 10 minutes +

Materials Copies of (a set of) text(s) (for example, see p.158)

Preparation Compose one or more exercises such as the one shown below and in the examples. If you want the exercise to be more challenging, do not present the chunks in the order that they should occur in the text.
Or to make the exercises easier you could: use familiar texts, insert marks to show where a chunk should go, and/or present the chunks in the order in which they should occur in the text.

in class Explain to your students that they should embed each chunk in the text so that sensible, natural wording results.

---

but in vain / at first / in desperation / let alone /
~~Once upon a time~~ / Nothing worked

Once upon a time

ʌ There was a king and queen whose son never went anywhere. He never

went out of the palace or to town. His parents thought that if they just

waited he would decide to go somewhere; but several years passed and he

still never went anywhere at all. Then they tried showing him pictures of

the beautiful world outside and bought him some running shoes. They gave

him maps and bus tickets. Finally they gave up and just ignored him. Now

he is king; but he still doesn't go anywhere.

4.11

Blanks with big fat hints

> Like all gap filling exercises, this one requires students to read intensively. It is designed to increase success rates without eliminating the need for students to engage in effortful recall.

Focus   Any kind of chunk

Level   Elementary +

Time   10 minutes

Materials   Copies of (a set of) gapped text(s) (for example, see pp.159-160)

Preparation   Make fill-in-the-blank exercises in which target chunks are given in abbreviated form, as shown in the examples, but ideally use a text that students have already worked with. Providing the initial letters is especially likely to trigger recall, although word endings can sometimes make good cues too.

You can make the hints even more potent by using line length to indicate the number of letters that have been omitted and by giving the final 's' in the case of a plural noun. This is what we have done in the example text.

Of course, you could increase success rates still more by also giving students a jumbled list of the words you have gapped out; but that really does increase the likelihood of success through sheer guesswork rather than the (more useful) mental effort otherwise required.

in class

Hand out or display the gapped text and ask your students to try to fill in the blanks.

RATIONALE

Blanks in place of whole words may fail to prompt recall of targeted chunks unless students have worked with these chunks ***very*** recently. Especially in the case of chunks that students have not met for some time, adding two- or three-letter prompts increases success rates without running a great risk that students can write correct answers by sheer guesswork: a degree of effort is still required to think of a correct answer. The higher success rates that go with big fat hints can be particularly important for motivational reasons, it being well known that success tends to be a better motivator than failure.

Finally, if the memory of a target chunk never comes to students' minds, then it will ***not*** be strengthened during a fill-in-the-blank exercise. True, students may find out what the correct chunks are when the exercise is corrected later on. But during this final stage of an activity, students – particularly those who have made more than their fair share of mistakes – are likely to be paying less attention than before.

Acknowledgement

We first found this technique being regularly used (but only with single word vocabulary) in tests of vocabulary size produced by Tom Cobb. His website, 'The Compleat Lexical Tutor' at http://www.lextutor.ca/, is a treasure trove of interesting links and tools for investigating L_2 vocabulary.

4.12

Student quizmasters

> This is an excellent way to get your students more involved in and committed to the practice of reviewing chunks regularly.

Focus Any kind of chunk

Level Intermediate +

Time 5 minutes or less

Materials None

Preparation Read the ideas in the Key for this activity.

in class

1. Elicit from your class all the different ways they know of in which a quiz can focus on chunk knowledge – e.g. using multiple choice questions and gap fills (for more ideas, see Key).

2. Explain that at the beginning of each future lesson, someone will have the job of quizzing the rest of the class on, say, five chunks that should be familiar to them. Add that the quizzes can be given orally or on paper, but stress that the quiz must be a real quiz in which students write the answers down on a sheet of paper.

3. Form a rota, perhaps by listing students' names in alphabetical order.

4. Give your students an example quiz.

VARIATIONS

1. Allow students to make and lead the quiz with *one* partner if they like.

2. Allow quiz-takers to team up with one partner.

Acknowledgement

This is a variation of an idea we learned from Paul Bress.

PHOTOCOPIABLE MATERIALS

Texts

Example text 1:
Pre-intermediate–
Intermediate

> A burglar who broke into a house in a city in central **Rus**sia
> changed his **mind** after seeing how **poor**ly **fur**nished it was.
> On a table, he left an amount of money **great**er than the average
> monthly pension.
> He **al**so left a written a**po**logy.

Example text 2:
Intermediate–
Upper intermediate

(the beginning
of a longer text)

> '**Head**scarf doesn't fit our **fun**ky image' says sa**lon** owner
> who turned **down** Muslim **sty**list
>
> The owner of a fashionable **hair** salon today de**nied** being a **rac**ist
> after turning **down** a headscarf-wearing **Mus**lim who applied for a
> **sty**list's job.
> Sarah Des**ros**iers, 3**2**, told a tri**bu**nal it was **vi**tal that **all** her staff
> show off "flam**boy**ant" haircuts at the **Wedge** sa**lon** in King's **Cross**.
> And Miss Des**ros**iers, from **Hack**ney,
> said 19-year-old Mrs Bushra Noah's **head**scarf
> was **out** of keeping with the "**ul**tra-modern, **ur**ban, **edg**y and **fun**ky"
> style of her **bus**iness.

Tip

Ask students to replace any difficult personal names with initials. So Miss Desrosiers would become Miss D.

Note

King's Cross and Hackney are districts in London.

Example text 3:
Advanced

(the beginning
of a longer text)

> ### A Waitress's Revenge
>
> After years **pan**dering to the whims of the rich and famous
> at New York's **best res**taurant,
> Phoebe Damrosch has **turn**ed the **ta**bles – by writing a **tell**-all **book**.
> "There are remarkably **few** truly **world** renowned restaurants.
> **And**, as I quickly came to **re**alise when I starred* **Per Se** in New
> York,
> "There are re**mar**kably few women who get to work in such

establishments at the **high**est level.

"I was the **on**ly female captain,   or head waiter,   at Per Se,

   and one of only **two** in the city's three-starred restaurants.

"As I dis**cov**ered,   the lofty reaches of **fine di**ning   can be a
   com**pell**ingly peculiar place.

"**Much** of what I witnessed –

and I have been assured it is the same at many top **Lon**don establishments –
   was worthy of a **film** script.

"Larger than life **char**acters;   bi**zarre** incidents.

"The stories I brought **home** with me

after a night waiting on some of the most ex**pen**sive tables in New York,

not to mention the **world**,

were what **prom**pted me   to write a **book** about my experiences."

* Line 5: 'starred' – i.e. when she marked a job ad in a newspaper with a star.

2.2 Examples

| Pretty woman, walking down the street | Don't make me cry |
| You look as lovely as can be | I'll treat you right |

Dialogues for Lesson 1

A: *When's dinner?*
B: *Soon.*
A: *What're we having?*
B: *The usual.*
A: *Can I help with anything?*
B: *You could lay the table.*
A: *Of course.*

Shopper: *How much is this?*
Shop assistant: *£4.99.*
Shopper: *I'll take it.*
Shop assistant: *Would you like it in a bag?*
Shopper: *No thanks.*

A: *Guess how old I am.*
B: *25.*
A: *Guess again.*
B: *I'm bad at guessing games. Just tell me.*
A: *I'm 30.*
B: *You look much younger.*
A: *Thank you.*

A: *What time is it?*
B: *It's time you bought a watch.*
A: *Very funny.*
B: ***I** thought so.*
A: *Can I borrow your mobile?*
B: *My phone?*
A: *I need to make a call.*
B: *Where's **yours**?*
A: *I forgot to bring it.*
B: *Oh, all right.*

A: *Can I borrow your car?*
B: *No way!*
A: *Why not?*
B: *You don't even know how to drive!*

A: *How do you write your name?*
B: *With a pen.*
A: *Very funny. I mean how do you **spell** it?*
B: *It's very long. I'll write it for you.*
A: *Thanks.*

Shopper: *Do you have these shoes in a size 10?*
Shop assistant: *I think so. Yes, here.*
Shopper: *Do you have them in brown?*
Shop assistant: *These **are** brown.*
Shopper: *I mean **dark** brown.*
Shop assistant: *Yes we do. Over here.*
Shopper: *Can I try them on?*
Shop assistant: *Of course.*

Student A: *Do you mind if I open the window? It's so stuffy in here.*
Student B: *I'll get cold.*
Student A: *A bit of fresh air won't kill us.*
Student B: *Please don't.*
Student A: *Why don't we change places?*
Student B: *OK.*

2.4

Worksheets

The Boy Who Cried Wolf (Aesop)

1 A shepherd boy had the job of watching over a flock of sheep near a village.
2 In one week, he called nearby villagers three times by crying out,
3 "Wolf! Wolf!"
4 When they *c. r. t. h.*, he laughed.
5 "I was just *h.f,*" he said.
6 And didn't they know it was boring being a shepherd *d. i. a. d. o.*?
7 *N.s.*, the villagers cursed him *l. and l.*,
8 One day, though, a wolf *did* come.
9 The shepherd boy yelled and yelled,
10 "Wolf*!* Help! *Wolf!*"
11 The villagers heard him, but no one came.
12 *A.a r.*, the whole flock of sheep was lost, all killed by the wolf.
13 As punishment, the boy's parents *b. h. bl. and bl.*
14 The moral? People may not believe liars even when they *t th t.*

Intermediate– Upper intermediate

1 A Spanish couple have got the **g. l.** from a judge
2 to evict their two sons, aged 19 and 20,
3 **o. th. gr. th.** living with them was **sh. h**.
4 The judge ruled that as the sons were adults,
5 their parents were **n. l. u. a. ob.**
6 to **pr**. them **w. r.** and **b.**
7 The sons were ordered to **cl. o. o.** the **f. h**
8 in a town in north east Spain.

104

Upper elementary

Tigers are big wild cats that live in Asia, not Africa. They are very rare now. Most of them live in India, but there are a few in some other countries. There are even a few tigers in the part of Russia that is near North Korea. Tigers have stripes. They like to swim. They eat other animals. Sometimes they attack people. But most people think tigers are beautiful even if they are dangerous.

Pre-intermediate

After celebrating her birthday, a Belarus woman felt sleepy and lay down on what she thought was the ground. During the night a train ran right over her and she didn't wake up. The place she picked to sleep was between the two rails of a train line. Doctors later said it was a good thing she didn't wake up and move while the train was passing over her. People who saw her lying on the train line in the morning thought she was dead and phoned the emergency services.

Intermediate

A true story

An Italian woman was in hospital to give birth. When the baby was born – and while the woman was still in bed – the husband gave the little boy the names of his favourite horse and jockey. So the boy's first name was the name of the jockey and his middle name was the name of the horse – or maybe vice versa. You see, the husband was passionate about betting on horse races. The hospital officials accepted the strange name because the man told them that his wife had agreed to it. But she hadn't agreed! In fact, she didn't know about these crazy names at all! She was furious at her husband when she found out what he had done. When she came out of hospital, she went to court and asked for a change of name – from the strange, 'horsey' names to names that were more traditional. Perhaps later she also asked for a divorce!

Intermediate

The Goose that laid Golden Eggs (Aesop, adapted)

A long time ago, a farming couple who lived in the countryside and raised geese made an exciting discovery. One of their geese had begun to lay a golden egg every Monday! As soon as the egg was laid, either the wife or the husband would take it to town, sell it, and begin spending the money. They began to spend so much money that soon they were in debt. They agreed that that one egg a week wasn't enough and so, one Tuesday, they killed it, hoping to get – who knows?— dozens or even hundreds of eggs! But inside the goose all they found was its insides. The moral? Being greedy for more can cost you what you already have.

Texts

Pre-intermediate
(some of the chunks are underlined, but there are other word partnerships worth remembering, e.g. *follow ... rules*).

Here are a few hair care rules you should follow without fail. Don't forget: wet hair can stretch and break. So never ever put ponytail bands in your hair after a shower or a swim. And when it's wet, don't brush your hair hard – not unless you want split ends. Another thing, sunlight is bad for wet hair, so don't even think about going outside to let your hair dry in the sun. If you're already outside, go into the shade! One more thing, keep that blow dryer away from the ends of your hair. This is a good way to damage them. Anyway, the ends will dry quite nicely on their own. Concentrate on drying the roots and middles, and leave the tips alone.

Intermediate

It Takes Two to Tango
A speed dating evening in an English village hall was called off when only one person showed up, a retired gentleman 73 years old. The event had been organised in response to complaints made by young single men that they were suffering from a lack of opportunities to meet young women. Quite a few had signed up for the evening, but apparently they lost their nerve and either stayed at home or went to the pub. It could be they missed out on a good time at the village hall.

These days, hardly anyone believes in vampires, but you'd never know it from watching Hollywood movies. Anyway, have you ever wondered how you can tell a vampire is a vampire? For one thing, they sleep during the day. This is because sunlight would be fatal to them. For another, a vampire has no reflection in a mirror. Finally, if a bag of rice falls on the floor, a vampire will have to count every single grain. Luckily, you can ward a vampire off with garlic, holy water or a cross, especially one made of silver. Another good thing is that a vampire can only come into your home if you invite it in yourself. So don't be too friendly to strangers!

Upper intermediate

Lottery winner Luke Pittard goes back to work ... at McDonald's
Lottery winner Luke Pittard has swapped slow living for fast food and gone back to work at McDonald's. The 25-year-old had been taking it easy since scooping £1.3m and quitting his job at the burger chain nearly two years ago. But after getting bored with life on the edge of the sofa he has gone back to his old job as a staff trainer. Father of three Luke earns £5.85 an hour and is up at the crack of dawn to get to work for his early shift at the Cardiff restaurant. "To be honest, there's only so much relaxing you can do. I'm only young and a bit of hard work never did anyone any harm," he told the BBC website.

Example gapped text

> **Survivor**
>
> .... endured .... hours (days…) in (on, under, near …) after being ....
> .... had given up hope for the .... , who was .... when .... was .... found in (on, under, near….) .... "If only .... had ....!" .... later said."

Text for Reviewing

Although our work at the quarry _____ show us that we were _____ prisoners, the authorities still _____ the _____ who once populated the island. Sometimes we would see a group of common-law prisoners working _____, and their warders would order them into the bushes so they would not see us _____. _____ mere _____ us might somehow affect their discipline. Sometimes _____ we could see a prisoner _____ in the ANC salute."

Nelson Mandela, *Long Walk to Freedom*, London: Abacus, p. 480

Sheet 1: Replies

All the time.	(Early) in the morning.	In the afternoon.
During the day.	In the evening.	(Late) at night.
In the (winter).	Now and then.	(Almost) never.
Whenever (I) can.	Never, if I can help it.	(Once…) a day.
Every day.	Every (two) days.	Could you say that again?
Whenever (I) need to. It varies.	Whenever (I) feel like it.	That's a difficult question.

Sheet 2: Questions

1 When do you have breakfast?
2 When do you go to bed?
3 When do you have a shower or bath?
4 When do you comb or brush your hair?
5 When does your heart beat?
6 When do you dream?
7 When do you dream about being here in class?
8 When did you have breakfast yesterday?
9 When do you eat bananas?
10 When does the sun come up?
11 When are children in school?
12 When do you have teeth in your mouth?
13 When is the moon full?
14 When are you going to go home today?
15 When do you eat chicken?
16 When do you see the stars?
17 When do you have fingers?
18 When is the weather the coldest?
19 When do you cook?
20 When do you read a newspaper?

21 When do you speak Chinese?
22 When do you work?
23 When do you think of the future?
24 When do you drink wine?
25 When do you think of your parents?
26 When do you cut your fingernails?
27 When do you *have* fingernails?
28 When do you put your shoes on?
29 When do ghosts move around?
30 When do you play tennis?
31 When do you blink?
32 When do cars crash?
33 When do you go shopping for food?
34 When do you tell the truth?
35 When do you eat rice?
36 When do tigers look for food?
37 When do elephants sleep?
38 When do mothers love their children?
39 When do want to be alone?
40 When do you get dressed for school or work?

Example transcript

An example of a gapped transcript for a between-listening gap fill exercise

First on BBC Radio 4, Andrew Luck-Baker discovers what factors play a .... in deciding whether our children will be male or female.

Most of us imagine it is completely 50/50 as to whether the new member of a family is a son or a daughter. But are the numbers of boys and girls in our families really down to the .... of a coin? In fact, it's not quite so simple.
For a ...., for every 100 girls born there are 105 boys. But also, you as an individual mother or father might have loaded the .... towards a son or a daughter right back at conception.

Ruth Mace, an anthropologist at University College London, was in Ethiopia in the year 2000, when the south of that country was hit by a severe food shortage. As part of a study on nutrition she looked .... the birth statistics of about 300 women caught up in the crisis.

'We thought it might be interesting to see whether the mothers' nutritional state was correlated in any .... with the sex of the baby that she had most recently produced. We did in fact find that there was a statistically significant effect. Mothers that had a higher body–mass ....
................, i.e. more body muscle, more body fat and also larger arm circumference, were more likely to have had their most recent birth be male than

female, and the converse of that.'

However, according to Valerie Grant of the University of Auckland, New Zealand, dominance in personality is the underlying factor:

'I came to notice that women who were a bit more dominant than others tended to have more boys. I did a series of tests of that over the years with groups of women in varying status and found that there was indeed a statistically .... result. Women who scored about 80% dominance on my personality test were about 80% more .... to conceive a son.

It may be that women who have strongly dominant characters are particularly suited to raising boys.'

Any theory which explains how and why individual parents are manipulating the odds over whether they have boys or girls might get a supportive boost if it could also account .... why at certain times the ratio of boys to girls born changes across entire populations. Something that happens towards the end of and just after war.
One analysis of German birth statistics from the months after the Second World War found 113.5 boys to every 100 girls.

If there is one thing everyone agrees on, is that there is still a long way to .... to make a coherent story out of all these data.

Texts

**Pre-intermediate-
Intermediate**

In rural Mexico, especially in the mountains, many people speak so-called Indian languages that are extremely different from Spanish. In 2007 a Mexican linguist said that one of these Indian languages had <u>died out</u>. This may seem strange if I also tell you that *two* men still spoke this language. So how could it have <u>died out</u>? The answer is that neither man ever spoke this language because they didn't like each other.

1   What is the opposite of *rural*? (If you don't know, find out!)

2   Here, does *Indian* mean 'of India'?

3   What do linguists study?

4   Does *die out* mean 'decrease' or does it mean 'disappear'?

5   In *die out*, what do you think *out* means?

One afternoon, a famous blind jazz piano player, George Shearing, came to a busy crossroads in a large city centre at rush hour. He stopped and waited for <u>a good Samaritan</u> – a kind, helpful stranger – to help him across the street. He waited and waited, but nobody offered to help him. Then, after quite a long time, someone finally felt his arm. It was another blind man who asked, "Would you be so kind as to help me across the street?" Tired of waiting for help himself, Shearing led the other blind man across. Later he said, "It was the biggest thrill of my life!"

1   What do you think is special about rush hour?

2   How many blind men are there in this story?

3   How do you think Shearing knew the other man was blind?

In 2007 an American man wanted to change one of the wheels on his car. Of course, before you can put new wheels on a car, you first have to remove the old ones. And to take off the old ones, you must be able to remove the 'nuts' from the 'bolts' that hold the wheel in place. But the man couldn't do this because he couldn't turn one of the nuts. It was too tight. So he <u>had a bright idea</u>. He got a rifle and tried to loosen the nut by shooting it. You will not be surprised to hear that soon afterwards the man was in a nearby hospital.

1   Why do you think the man wanted to change the wheel?

2   What tool do you use to turn nuts?

3   About the phrase *had a bright idea* … is it sarcastic here, or not?

4   What's the opposite of *tight*?

5   Why did an ambulance come?

6   Draw a picture of a bolt and a nut to show when you retell this story later.

There is a famous exchange of words between the politicians Winston Churchill and Lady Astor, who disagreed about many things. One weekend they were both staying at Blenheim Palace, where Churchill had been born. Lady Astor and Churchill were <u>at each other's throats</u> the whole time. Finally, Lady Astor said, "Winston, if I were your wife, I'd put poison in your coffee."
Churchill replied, "Nancy, if I were your husband, I'd drink it."

1   About how long ago do you think this happened?

2   If you want to strangle someone, which part of their body do you put your hands around?

3   Do you think *be at each other's throats* has a friendly meaning?

4   Which did Churchill mean – that if Lady Astor was his wife, he would feel so happy he would love to drink her coffee? Or so unhappy he would want to die?

During a newspaper strike, someone told the ageing American movie star Bette Davis that there were rumours that she had died. Davis said, "Me, die during a newspaper strike?! <u>I wouldn't dream of it</u>!"

1   Was Bette Davis young at the time of the newspaper strike?

2   Do you think this was before or after TV and the internet became so popular compared to newspapers?

3   Why do you think she said she would refuse to die during a newspaper strike?

In a small city in the USA a man walked into a fast food restaurant early in the morning, showed a gun, and demanded money. The employee behind the counter – a teenager – said he couldn't open the till without a food order. When the <u>would-be</u> robber ordered onion rings, the teenager told him they weren't available for breakfast. The man, frustrated, walked away.

1   When the would-be robber demanded money, what do you think he said?

2   What do you think a 'till' is?

3   Do you think a *would-be robber* is someone who has succeeded in robbing a business of some kind or who wants to succeed in robbing one?

4   Do you think the teenager was brave and clever?

There is a story about the Canadian ice hockey team in Russia in 1972. Some of the Canadians thought that the Russians might try to find out secrets about their game plans by putting listening devices in their hotel rooms. So some of the Canadians began to look for hidden microphones. In the middle of one room they found a round piece of metal on the floor under a rug. Maybe this is what they thought: "If we remove it, <u>what harm can it</u> do?" A second after they <u>had removed</u> the piece of metal, they heard a crash in the room just below them. It was the noise was made by a chandelier crashing to the floor.

1   Did the Canadians find a real hidden microphone?

2   What was the round piece of metal?

3   When people say *What harm can it do?* do you think it's (a) when they think an action may have a good result and probably will have no bad result or (b) when they know for sure how to solve a problem?

Some years ago, in a city in Italy, a street musician was playing music from an opera composed by Pietro Mascagni. By chance, he was playing exactly in front of Mascagni's apartment, *and* he was playing the music much too slowly. After a while, the composer couldn't tolerate it any more. It really got on his nerves to hear his own music played so terribly. So he went down into the street, said to the musician, "I am Mascagni," and showed him how to play the music at the correct speed. Then the composer went back up to his apartment. But later, he heard the street musician playing the same music, still too slowly! Mascagni went down into the street again and saw that now the musician had a sign beside him which said *Student of Mascagni*.

1   If something *gets on your nerves* does it (a) make you smile?, (b) make you feel irritated?, or (c) make you feel kind and sensitive?

2   Was the street musician really one of Mascagni's students?

3   The composer didn't like the musician's sign. But why not?

Even when he was quite young, the writer Mark Twain was famous for the number of cigars he smoked, more than 100 a month. He said that when he was a small boy he tried chewing tobacco but that made him sick. So when he was 8 years old, he took up smoking cigars. Someone once asked him what brand of cigars he smoked at that age. Twain answered that the brand he smoked were probably not very good "or the previous smoker would not have thrown it away so soon".

1   At what age did Mark Twain try chewing tobacco?

2   Why did he change to cigars?

3   When he was a boy, how did he get his cigars?

4   Were they new?

5   Were they whole?

6   Do you think 'take up' might be the opposite of 'give up'?

A young travelling preacher arrived in a new town. That night, he was going to talk about God and religion in a local church. Before that, however, he decided to walk around town and see the sights. One thing he wanted to do was mail a letter. He saw a young boy and asked him where he could mail a letter. The boy told him where the post office was. The preacher said, "Thank you. And, by the way, if you come to the church tonight, you'll find out how you can get to heaven." The boy answered that no, he wasn't going to come. "Why not?" asked the preacher. "Well," said the boy, "Get to heaven? You didn't even know how to get to the post office!"

1   What sights do you think you could see in a typical small town in your country about 70 years ago?

2   Do you like little boys of this kind?

A famous politician, Robert Kennedy, was <u>born with a silver spoon in his mouth</u> and so was accustomed to people doing things for him. For this reason – although he was *very* rich – he almost never carried money with him. Instead, whenever he went anywhere, he expected the people he was with to pay. One Sunday, he was at church with a friend. Of course, at the end of a church service everyone should put some money into a 'collection' plate that is passed from person to person. When the Kennedy's friend put in one dollar, Kennedy whispered to him, "Don't you think I would be more generous than that?"

1   Do poor families usually feed children with silver spoons?

2   When his friends and acquaintances paid for things for him, do you think he ever paid them back?

3   What would you have said to this politician if you had been one of his friends?

4   Do you ever put money in a collection plate or anything like that?

5   If so, where?

2.13 Jumbled sentences

One day in a café, …

But the next day, they both apologised and <u>made up</u>.
One day he <u>popped the question</u>.
The Big Day came and they <u>tied the knot</u>.
During the next few weeks, they <u>hung out</u> a lot <u>together</u>.
He decided to <u>chat her up</u>.
But not long after that, they <u>had a row</u> and <u>broke off their engagement</u>.
He <u>caught her eye</u> and vice versa.
How are they <u>getting on</u> now? Well, <u>so far so good</u>.
They gradually <u>fell in love</u>.
They <u>hit it off</u>.
They <u>set a date for</u> the wedding.
She said "Yes" and that meant they were engaged.

2.14 Master list

Situational clichés and explanations
Delete items you don't want to work with.

1	*Ta-dah!*	Said when you are showing off a new garment as if you were a model … or when you've just made something, and you show it off as if you're a magician who has just pulled it out of a hat.
2	*Hey presto!*	Said when you've been showing someone how to make something and at the end you show off the finished product. It means, "Look! Here it is! Finished!"
3	*Oops-a-daisy!*	Said encouragingly to someone, a toddler for example, who stumbles and nearly falls.
4	*I'm having a senior moment.*	You might say this if you've just been forgetful, like old people are supposed to be.
5	*Small world!*	Said especially when you are in a place far away from home and you meet someone from your local area.
6	*It takes two to tango.*	To indicate that, of two people involved in a scandal, both are to blame.
7	*He couldn't organise a piss-up in a brewery* (A 'piss-up' is a drunken party.)	= 'He is incapable of organising anything.'
8	*It figures.*	Re (= regarding) a bad act on the part of someone of whom you have, for some time, had a low opinion. It means, "I'm not at all surprised."
9	*Don't hold your breath.*	To say that something isn't going to happen soon, or at all. E.g. 'Don't hold your breath until I agree to do it.' = 'I won't do it soon, if ever.' (A bit sarcastic.)
10	*I'm having a bad hair day.*	= 'Nothing's going right for me today and I feel out of sorts.'
11	*Another one bites the dust.*	Said when you hear of yet another case of someone failing, quitting, being fired, or dying. (From cowboy movies when a shot rider falls off his horse face first in the dust, dead.)
12	*What goes around comes around*	People who treat others badly will eventually get treated badly in return.
13	*It's a Catch-22 situation.*	From Joseph Heller's novel **Catch-22**, we say this about a situation in which someone has to accomplish two actions but each action is dependant on the other action being completed first. A familiar example is when someone trying to get their first job after leaving school finds that they cannot get a job without work experience but cannot gain experience without a job.
14	*Fingers crossed!*	To express the hope that everything will turn out all right despite a possibility of the opposite.
15	*The less said the better.*	A lot of criticisms could be made but you think it would be better not to voice them.

16	*Speak of the devil …*	When someone about whom you've been speaking about appears on the scene. It's usually used of someone you know quite well, and like.
17	*Beginner's luck.*	When someone who is inexperienced at something succeeds at it brilliantly.
18	*Good timing.*	When someone does something at the perfect moment.
19	*One of these days …* (said grimly)	= e.g., "One of these days, you'll get your come-uppance." I.e. this may be a threat (to someone) or a prophecy (about someone) that they will some day get a well deserved punishment.
20	*Good riddance!*	To say that you are glad about the departure or disappearance of someone or something you don't approve of. (The full expression is 'Good riddance to bad rubbish!')
21	*Still waters run deep.*	You say this about a quiet, modest person who you learn has just done something extraordinary, in order to indicate your pleased surprise that s/he could have done such a daring or exciting thing.
22	*Say when.*	To invite someone to tell you when to stop pouring – when, e.g., you are about to refill their wine glass. (The response is Whoa! or When!)
23	*You're getting warm.*	Said in a guessing game or find-the-object game to indicate that the guesser/searcher is getting near the answer/object.
24	*If you say so.*	To indicate superficial acceptance of a suggestion or command, but underlying disagreement.
25	*I've lost my thread.*	I've forgotten what I wanted to say.
26	*So far so good.*	To say that things are going well in a situation where failure is a strong possibility.
27	*I haven't the foggiest.*[UK]	= 'I haven't the foggiest idea.' = 'I have no idea at all.'
28	*And Bob's your uncle.*[UK]	When you give instructions to someone, you can finish by saying this in order to emphasise that the rest of the process will be quick and easy.
29	*Sod's law.*[UK]	= 'If something can go wrong, it will.' This is what British people usually say; US English is *Murphy's law*.

Other clichés: *Likely story; Great minds think alike; Famous last words; Touch wood* [UK] / *Knock wood* [US]; *You too; Help yourself; Dig in; How long is a piece of string?; Be my guest; Knock yourself out* [US]; *I don't mind if I do; I wouldn't put it past (him); Close but no cigar; Fat chance!; And pigs might fly; Fire away!; As if!; The more the merrier; The sooner the better; Jackpot!; Do you mind?!; Are you taking the Mickey)?* [UK] *You 'avin' a laugh?* [UK] *Put a sock in it!; Let's not rake over the past; Never say die; That's just sour grapes; There's (only) one way to find out.*

Initials Prompts for Reviewing

1 When you are showing off a new garment, etc. (Hint: *Ta-...*)

2 If you're showing someone how to make something and then you show them the finished result, maybe you say this. (Hint: *H, p.*)

3 To a small child who's stumbled. (Hint: *Oops-a-...*)

4 When you've just been forgetful. (Hint: *senior*)

5 = "What a coincidence, meeting you here!" (Hint: *small*)

6 = "It's not the fault of just one of them." (Hint: *tango*)

7 = "He is incapable of organising anything properly." (Hint: *brewery*)

8 Re a bad act on the part of someone of whom you have, for some time, had a low opinion. (Hint: *I. f.*)

9 = "Don't wait for it to happen, because you might have to wait for a long time" (Hint: *breath*)

10 = Nothing is going quite right for me today. (Hint: *Maybe you should change your shampoo.*)

11 = *One more down* (Hint: *dust*).

12 = *The wrong you do will come back to you in the end.* (Hint: *round.*)

13 What you may say, e.g. if you can't get a job unless you have work experience and you can't get experience unless you have a job. (Hint: 22)

14 To express the hope that everything will turn out all right despite a possibility of the opposite. (Hint: F.c.*!*)

15 A lot of criticisms could be made but you think it would be better not to voice them. Hint: *Less, Better*

16 When someone about whom you've been speaking appears on the scene. (Sp. o. th. D.)

17 What someone may when a new team member has succeeded brilliantly (Hint: *luck*)

18 When someone does something at the perfect moment. Hint: *G.t.*

19 A threat (to someone) or prophecy (about someone) that they will some day get well deserved punishment. (Hint: *One of these...*)

20 About someone's welcome departure. (Hint: *G. r.!*)

21 Re a quiet person who you hear has just done something extraordinary. (Hint: *deep*)

22 = "Tell me when to stop pouring." (Hint: *S. w.*)

23 = You're close to finding what you're looking for. (Hint: *temperature*)

24 To indicate superficial acceptance but underlying disagreement. (Hint: *If you...*)

25 = "I've forgotten what I was in the middle of saying." (Hint: *thread*)

26 = "No problems yet." (Hint: *S. f., s. g.*)

27 = "I have no idea." (Hint: *fog)*

28 The same as the one of Mr Murphy

29 When you give instructions to someone, you can finish by saying this ... in order to emphasise that the result will be quick and easy. (Hint: *Bob*)

Handouts

Things that smell (Add or delete items as appropriate to the level of your class)

1 freshly baked bread
2 hand lotion
3 the air on a frosty morning
4 an outdoor barbecue
5 an ocean beach
6 a Chinese restaurant
7 a camp fire
8 a Christmas tree
9 the water of a fresh mountain stream
10 burning feathers or hair
11 boxes of apples
12 breath that smells of garlic
13 a dairy farm or cow shed
14 a deep, dark forest
15 freshly mown grass
16 newly fallen snow
17 chicken frying in a pan
18 garden soil when you've just turned it over with a spade
19 a new book
20 crushed orange peel
21 a hay barn
22 laundry on the clothes line on a hot summer's day
23 burning incense (e.g. in a church or temple)
24 when it rains in summer after a long hot dry period
25 a fast-food restaurant specialising in hamburgers
26 burning rubbish
27 a rainforest
28 an Indian restaurant
29 thick sea fog
30 a car that smells of cigarette smoke
31 the inside of a sea shell
32 burning leaves

33 horse stables
34 strong coffee
35 a hospital corridor
36 cold, clean air before it snows
37 a ripe, garden-grown tomato
38 a match which has just been struck
39 petrol fumes (gasoline fumes[US])
40 freshly split wood
41 a candle just after you've blown it out
42 a just-sharpened pencil
43 toothpaste
44 old saddles and other leather things
45 a stable with horses in it
46 nail polish remover
47 an indoor swimming pool
48 crushed rose petals
49 household bleach
50 wood smoke in the autumn
51 suntan lotion
52 fresh paint
53 a pine tree
54 someone's hair
55 new magazines
56 fish and chips
57 a saw mill
58 pipe tobacco
59 a wet dog
60 crushed eucalyptus leaves
61 an underground station (subway station[US])
62 fumes from a diesel bus
63 garlic being fried

Note

A few of these do not include a chunk; they are there to make the activity work better.

Possible Responses Sheet (about smells)

Positive	*Good.* *Mmm!* *I like that.* *I just love that!*
Negative	*I don't like that at all.* *I hate that!* *Ugh! Yuk! Ick!* *Disgusting!* *Revolting!*
Neutral	*Nothing.* *Zero.* *That does nothing for me.* *Nothing one way or the other.*
Memories and Associations	*Ah, that reminds me of (when) …* *I associate that with …*

3.2 List and Reactions Sheet

List of sounds for upper intermediate
(Add or delete items as appropriate to the level of your class.)

1 a ticking clock
2 water coming to the boil in a kettle
3 the clatter of dishes and pots & pans in a kitchen
4 screeching tyres
5 an ambulance siren
6 children playing in a playground at a school
7 cow bells
8 the rumble of distant thunder
9 the pitter-patter of rain on a car roof
10 distant church bells
11 seagulls screeching
12 cows mooing in the distance
13 sheep baaing
14 someone eating with their mouth open
15 a football game
16 a party in a nearby house or flat
17 an alarm clock going off
18 water lapping against a dock or the side of a boat
19 a doorbell ringing
20 bees buzzing
21 footsteps crunching on a gravel path
22 someone brushing their teeth
23 the crackling of a campfire
24 fireworks banging and whizzing in the sky
25 lions roaring
26 songbirds early in the morning
27 crows cawing in the distance
28 airplanes overhead
29 schoolchildren playing outside
30 elephants trumpeting
31 flies buzzing around inside a room
32 someone reading a newspaper
33 a train crossing a bridge
34 water plunging over a waterfall
35 airplanes taking off
36 blinds rattled by a breeze coming in through an open window
37 car horns honking in city traffic
38 crashing waves
39 popping corks
40 distant drums
41 chickens clucking

Personal Reactions Sheet (sounds)

Positive	That's a sound I like because … For me, that's positive because …
Negative	For me, that's negative because … I hate that!
Neutral	Nothing. I never hear that. I don't know what that is. Nothing one way or the other.
Memories and Associations	… (because) I associate that with … … (because) when I think of that it reminds me of …

3.3 Figurative manner-of-movement expressions

Pre-intermediate

1 *Arms up. Stretch!*
2 *Arms down. Now swing your arms.*
3 *Imagine you have a book in your hands, an imaginary book. Look at it. You can see the front; it's red and green. Turn it over and look at the back. Turn it over again and look at the front.*
4 *Snap your fingers. Oh, the book's gone – it's disappeared. Magic!*
5 *Lean left. Now stand up straight again.*
6 *Step back. Now step forward again.*
7 *Raise your arms again.*
8 *Arms down. Yes, lower them.*
9 *Oh, no! Someone has just thrown a tomato at you! Here it comes … straight at your face! Duck! – Ha! Ha! Missed me!*
10 *Arms up! Yes, let's raise them again.*
11 *Arms down. Yes, lower them. Now, click, or 'snap' your fingers!*
12 *Oh, someone has asked you a difficult question. Scratch your head.*
13 *Your hands are cold. Rub them together.*
14 *Oh, it's time to sit down and get back to work.*

Intermediate
(Also, recycle items from the pre-intermediate list)

1 *Wriggle like a worm! OK, enough of that.*
2 *Oh, there's a bug on your shoulder! Flick it off!*
3 *Oh, there's another one. Smack it!*
4 *Got it! Blow it off.*
5 *There's an imaginary flower. Pick it. Sniff it. Lovely. Very fragrant … in an imaginary sort of way.*
6 *Spin around left! Spin around right!*
7 *Look out! Here comes that tomato again. Duck!*
8 *Here comes another one! Dodge left! And another one! Dodge right!*
9 *And another one! Catch it! Throw it back!*

Upper intermediate
(Also, recycle items from the pre-intermediate and intermediate lists)

1 *You think you're dreaming. Pinch yourself. No, it's not a dream – you're at the opera. The man next to you is snoring. Nudge him, like this. Good, he wakes up.*
2 *Suddenly the opera changes into a haunted house and you're all alone.*
3 *There's a box. Open it. Slowly, slowly. Out pops a ghost! Gasp! Flinch!*
4 *Here comes a bat flying straight at your face! Ward it off! Here comes another one! Ward it off!*
5 *Oh, now suddenly you're playing rugby in the haunted house. A ghost tries to tackle you. Ward it off! Hooray! You score!*
6 *Your mobile rings. It's me saying it's time to get back to work. You wake up. You were dreaming after all.*

Pre-intermediate

1 Sometimes it's necessary to <u>make a snap decision</u>.
2 Fishermen are famous for <u>stretching the truth</u> about the fish they catch.
3 In a shop, when <u>prices are lowered</u>, that's called a sale.
4 I don't know what to do yet. I'm still <u>turning</u> things <u>over in my mind</u>.

Intermediate
(with some recycling of verbs introduced at a lower level)

1 He's famous for his <u>sudden mood swings</u>. I wonder what mood he'll be in when we meet him today.
2 Please <u>don't raise your voice</u> like that. This is supposed to be a friendly discussion.
3 The prime minister <u>ducked a question</u> about the war.
4 Some people are experts at <u>wriggling out of their responsibilities</u>.
5 Two glasses of champagne, and <u>my head is spinning</u>.
6 The police investigated the crime but they didn't look deep enough. They just <u>scratched the surface</u>.

Upper intermediate
(with some recycling of verbs introduced at a lower level)

1 If the 'fare' is the money you pay for a train, bus or taxi trip, what do you suppose a '<u>fare dodger</u>' is?
2 You can operate this machine with a <u>flick of your wrist</u>. A child could do it.
3 Conservative politicians often attempt to <u>sway voters</u> with promises of tax cuts.
4 I'm <u>feeling the pinch</u> financially.
5 Some people believe that taking lots of vitamin C will help you <u>ward off</u> colds.
6 She succeeded in her <u>last-gasp attempt</u> to pass her medical exam.
7 The audience was disappointed when all three speakers <u>dodged every question</u> about their views on immigration.
8 Politicians may avoid <u>tackling</u> the most difficult <u>problems,</u> and so let them get worse from year to year.
9 She never <u>flinched from her duty</u>, neither when a policewoman nor later when she was in the army.
10 Reducing interest rates may <u>nudge</u> an economy <u>into action</u> because people will find money cheaper to borrow and so they will buy more.

Note

Manner-of-action verbs express a general kind of movement carried out in a particular manner. For example, the meaning of the manner-of-action verb 'slap' can be analyzed as follows:

Slap[-ped] ➡ *General* action: 'hit' + Manner: 'hard, with the palm of the hand'

These verbs are often found in Germanic languages such as English (and in Slavic languages too). Because the verbs are so imagistic, they are often used in figurative expressions such as the ones ones above, especially in newspapers. But in Latin–based languages, such verbs are less numerous and play much less of a role in communication. Students who speak these languages can particularly benefit from activities which show how these verbs are used in English.

3.4 Worksheet

Weather condition	Advantage	Disadvantage
1 *a rainy day*	May be good for farmers	Unpleasant if you want to go to the beach
2 *a heavy frost*		
3 *a chilly wind*		
4 *a misty morning*		
5 *a slight haze*		
6 *a breezy day*		
7 *a loud clap of thunder*		
8 *a bright flash of lightning*		
9 *a strong gale*		
10 *blue sky*		
11 *changeable weather*		

3.4 Example Sentences

1 Because of all the terrible things he'd written about people in his hometown in his last novel, he <u>got a frosty reception</u> when he returned there to give a speech.

2 It was a sad movie. By the end, almost everyone was <u>misty-eyed</u>; and some were actually crying.

3 I've read that book, but so long ago that now I only have <u>a</u> very <u>hazy memory</u> of what it's about.

4 All his jokes elicited <u>gales of laughter</u>. By the end, some people had laughed so hard they had tears streaming down their faces.

5 They say that <u>lightning never strikes twice in the same place</u>, but I read about someone who won the national lottery two times!

6 You look <u>bright and breezy</u> today.

7 After their boss told them that none of them was working hard enough, <u>the atmosphere</u> in the meeting turned <u>frosty</u>.

8 As soon as she stopped singing, the audience demonstrated their approval with <u>thunderous applause.</u>

9 The news of his death so young <u>struck me like a thunderclap.</u>

10 When he told her the news, she stood there <u>thunderstruck</u>. Obviously, it was the last thing she had expected to hear.

11 They keep about 20,000 Euros in a bank account they never touch. They say it's their <u>rainy day fund</u>.

12 Our director of training is going to lead a series of seminars on creativity. The first one is entitled '<u>Blue sky thinking</u>'.

13 Some people are known for their <u>changeable moods</u>.

Review Sheet

1 Because of all the terrible things he'd written about people in his hometown in his last novel, he got a frosty re.............tion when he returned there to give a speech.

2 It was a sad movie. By the end, almost everyone was .....isty-......ed; and some were actually crying.

3 I've read that book, but so long ago that now I only have a very ....zy ....ory of what it's about.

4 All his jokes elicited .....ales of l.............ter. By the end, some people had laughed so hard they had tears streaming down their faces.

5 They say that ....tning never str............. tw............. in the s............. pl............. , but, you know, I read about someone who won the national lottery two times!

6 You look ....ight and br.............y today. You must be feeling a lot better!

7 After their boss told them that none of them was working hard enough, the atmosphere in the meeting turned fr..............

8 As soon as she stopped singing, the audience demonstrated their approval with th.................ous app............. .

9 The news of his death so young str............. me like a th.......................lt.

10 When he told her the news, she stood there th.............str............. . Obviously, it was the last thing she had expected to hear.

11 They keep about 20,000 Euros in a bank account they never touch. They say it's their r.............y d............. ....nd.

12 Our director of training is going to lead a series of seminars on creativity. The first one is entitled 'Bl............. sk...... thinking'.

13 Some people are known for their ch.......................e moods.

3.5 Handout

Upper Intermediate Review Sheet for Device Words.

1 For chopping down trees or splitting firewood.

2 For digging holes with.

3 An egg-timer is a small one of these.

4 Farmers use this on fences so cows and horses can't escape.

5 This is something on which you can clean your shoes before you go into a house. On it, you may see the word 'Welcome'.

6 If you work in a park, you may use one of these to collect fallen leaves. If you work for a casino at a roulette table, you use one of these to collect players' money,

7 You can use one of these to arrange your hair. It can easily fit into a pocket.

8 You can use one of these to keep a door open. If you cut a circular cake into pieces, each piece is usually this shape.

9 For breaking big rocks with.

10 You may need one of these to keep your trousers up.

11 You may use one of these if you want to pour liquid into a bottle without spilling any of it.

12 This has the same function as a nail; but you don't hit it, you turn it.

13 Before you use flour to make bread, you put it through one of these.

14 For rowing a boat with.

Figurative Idioms Sheet

1 *I've got a memory like a sieve.*

2 *I used to be as thin as a rake.*

3 *Their business is doing well. They're really raking in the cash.*

4 *He's as diplomatic as a sledgehammer.*

5 *Petrol prices have gone up again. We're going to have to tighten our belts.*

6 *Could be hard times ahead. They've axed 1,000 jobs at the local chemical plant.*

7 *You think you can treat me like a doormat! I'm leaving!!*

8 *Some people just can't call a spade a spade. Do you suppose they're afraid that if they give an honest opinion they might conceivably offend somebody somewhere on planet earth?*

9 *Jane's mother tried to drive a wedge between Jane and her husband.*

10 *The news of the crash hit me like a sledgehammer.*

11 *Don't pay any attention to anything he says. He's got a screw loose.*

12 *In around 1900, an hour-glass figure was considered the ideal for ladies.*

13 *If you let one student come late to class, that can be the thin end of the wedge. Soon two will come late. Then four, then six, and then everybody.*

14 *The police combed the area for the missing child.*

15 *The government is funnelling extra money into childcare.*

16 *Barbed comments can hurt people's feelings.*

17 *Nobody asked you to put your oar in*[UK]*! If I want to hear what you've got to say, I'll ask you.*

Additional idioms for advanced learners: ***He knows a lot about theory but nothing about <u>the nuts and bolts</u>*** = the practical details; ***<u>Throw a spanner into the works</u>***[UK] = sabotage; ***It was <u>a tough row to hoe</u>*** = a difficult job; ***After the battle, the victors <u>conducted mopping-up operations</u>*** = tried to eliminate remaining small pockets of resistance.

3.6 Handouts

Handout 1: Basic information

A Typical 'Hand' Of Five Card Stud Poker from Beginning to End

1 The dealer **shuffles** (= mixes up) the cards.

2 The players **ante** (= they each put a chip in the centre of the table). (Pronunciation: /ˈænti/)

3 The dealer **deals** (= gives) 2 cards to each player, 1 card face up, and 1 face down.

4 The players **bet** with cash or **chips** (i.e. they put more money in the centre of the table; but players who don't like their cards can quit).

5 The dealer deals a third card, face up, to everyone still playing.

6 More betting.

7 The dealer deals a fourth card, face up, to everyone still playing.

8 More betting.

9 The dealer deals a fifth card, face up, to everyone still playing.

10 More betting, for the last time.

11 Now, all **the chips are 'down'** (i.e. in the centre of the table).

12 The players show their cards by laying them on the table, face up. This is called **the showdown**. The player with the best 'hand' (i.e. the best cards) wins.

13 The winner takes the **pot** (i.e. all the money in the centre of the table).

Handout 2: More basic information

Basic Card-playing Vocabulary

1 A **pack**UK/**deck**US of cards = a complete set of cards, usually 52.

2 Your **hand** is the cards that you have been dealt.

3 Four **suits** ➡: spades ♠, hearts ♥, diamonds ♦, clubs ♣.

4 Four **aces**; twelve **court cards** ie 4 kings, 4 queens, 4 knaves/jacks.

5 A **joker** is a wild card. In some games it can be used as any card you want it to be.

6 **Trumps** is the highest suit in a particular game. If no suit is designated as trumps, spades is by default the most powerful suit, so that, for example, a 10 of spades ♠ beats a 10 of any other suit.

7 To **stack the deck** = to secretly arrange the cards so that your opponents get bad cards.

8 To **tip your hand** = to hold your cards (accidentally or on purpose) so that the person next to you can see them.

9 The **stakes** = the money you are risking. A high stakes game is one in which the players can bet (and win or lose) a lot of money.

10 **Chips** are coin-shaped objects typically made of plastic. They represent money and are what gamblers use to ante and bet. Blue chips are, traditionally, the most valuable.

11 A card '**in the hole**' is a card which is turned face down and so hidden from other players' view. **An ace in the hole** = an ace that you can see but no one else can; it's a secret high card.

Handout 3: Idioms and meanings for cutting up into jumbled strips

1 He <u>plays his cards close to his chest</u>.   *keeps his plans secret*

2 It's time for everyone to
 <u>lay all their cards on the table</u>.   *say what they are thinking*

3 The PM has announced <u>a cabinet re-shuffle</u>.   *a re-organisation*

4 She didn't just win – she <u>won in spades!</u>   *emphatically, clearly, by a wide margin*

5 It's <u>not on the cards</u>^{UK}/<u>in the cards</u>^{US}.   *not possible*

6 We've got <u>the winning hand</u>.   *most or all of the advantages*

7 I've got <u>an ace in the hole/up my sleeve</u>.   *a secret advantage*

8 She always <u>turns up trumps</u> in the end.   *does a great job when it really matters*

9 You can always rely on her
 <u>when the chips are down</u>.   *in a deciding, end-game, situation*

10 Mathematics is not <u>my strong suit</u>.   *my best talent*

11 He <u>threw in his hand</u>. = He <u>folded (his hand)</u>.   *gave up, quit*

12 We're holding <u>all the trumps / aces / high cards</u>.   *all the advantages*

13 He's <u>the joker in the pack/the wild card</u>.   *the unpredictable one*

14 Do you mind if I <u>chip in</u>?   *contribute* (i.e. pay part of a bill, or add s'thing into a conversation)

15 The cards <u>are stacked against us</u>.   *Things are against us.*

16 It's time to <u>up the ante</u>.
 = It's time to <u>raise the stakes</u>.   *increase the investment and so increase the risk.*

17 The PM had <u>a showdown</u> with his chancellor <br> over the issue of interest rates.   *a decisive confrontation*

18 She <u>tipped her hand</u>.   *gave a hint about her intentions (accidentally or on purpose)*

19 If you <u>play your cards right</u>, you might succeed.   *make good use of your resources & opportunities*

20 Try to <u>keep a poker face</u> during the negotiation.   *not show your thoughts or feelings*

21 Being a very conservative investor,
 I only invest in <u>blue chip</u> companies.   *highly valued*

Handout 4

A story with both figurative and literal chunks.

(Target items are underlined and numbered.)

Jack and Jill like playing poker. They play with the same acquaintances a few times a week. At the beginning of each night, the stakes are low[1] with a maximum bet of only £1. But after a couple of hours of play, J&J and the other players always decide to raise the stakes[2] to a maximum of £50 per bet.

Why do J&J play with *acquaintances* and not with friends? The reason is they have no friends, and the reason for that is that they both love money, love winning, and will cheat in order for the money to be theirs. That's right; honesty is not their strong suit[3]. For instance, they both like to keep an ace up their sleeve[4]. (It is not easy to cheat by pulling an ace out of your sleeve and putting it into your hand, but J&J cheat in other ways too.)

One night, this happened: the dealer had dealt the cards and Jack had all the aces[5] and was certain to win. He played his cards close to his chest[6] so that no one could see what they were. He gave Jill a secret sign that he had the winning hand[7] and she threw in her hand[8]. (Because they were married, they didn't like to win each other's money.) But all the other players had good hands too, and stayed in the game. After the betting had finished (when all the chips were down[9]) came the showdown[10]. In short, everybody had laid all their cards on the table[11] so that everyone could see who had the best hand. Jack, of course, had four aces plus the joker (i.e. 5 aces!) and so he reached for the money in the middle of the table – but as he did so yet another ace fell out of his shirt-sleeve. Another player – who was sitting next to Jill -- pulled a pistol out of her handbag, pointed it at Jack, and said, "Don't touch that money, you cheating rat! Now listen. If you stand up, leave *all* your money on the table, and walk out that door, I won't call the police."

"Call the police?!" Jack said. "You wouldn't do that. It's not on the cards[12]."

"And *why* is it not on the cards?" asked the woman.

"Because," Jack said, "the police would want to know why you carry a pistol in your handbag. Listen. I'm going to lay all my cards on the table[13] right now. Yes, I've been cheating you all. Yes, you caught me tonight. But what are you going to do about it? Nothing! Why? Because I have one more ace up my sleeve[14]."

"And what ace is that?" asked the woman.

"The ace up my sleeve is that I know you're afraid to shoot *and* afraid to call the police!" said Jack. And with that Jill shouted, "Grab the money, Jack!" He did, and J&J ran out the door, ran down the street, jumped in their car, and drove off. "Jill, you're a good woman to have around when the chips are down![15]" said Jack.

Jill replied, "Thanks for the compliment, but from now on, let me be the only one who carries an ace up her sleeve[16]."

Handout 5: First Review Sheet

1   He plays his cards **cl**_____ to his **ch**_____. = *keeps his plans secret*

2   It's time for everyone to **l**_____ all their cards on the **t**_____. = *say what they are thinking*

3   The PM has announced a cabinet **re**_____**uffle**. = *a re-organisation*

4   She didn't just win, she won in ____**ades**. = *emphatically, clearly, by a wide margin*

5   It's not on the **c**_____. = *not possible*

6   We've got the **w**_____ **h**_____. = *most or all of the advantages*

7   I've got an _____ in the hole / up my sleeve. = *have a secret advantage*

8   She always **comes up** ____**umps** in the end. = *does a great job when it really matters*

9   You can always rely on her when the _____ are down. = *in a deciding, end-game, situation.*

10 Mathematics is not my **s**_____ **s**_____. = *my best talent*

11 He threw in his **h**_____. = He **f**_____ (his **h**_____). = *gave up, quit*

12 We're holding all the **tr**_____ / **a**_____ / **high c**_____. = *all the advantages*

13 He's the __**oker** in the **p**_____= the **w**_____ **card**. = *the unpredictable one*

14 Do you mind if I ____**ip in**? = *contribute (i.e. pay part of a bill or add something into a conversation)*

15 The cards are ___**acked against us**. = *things are against us*

16 It's time **to up the a**_____. / It's time to **raise the** ___**akes**. = *increase the investment and so increase the risk.*

17 The PM had **a sh**_____ with his minister of finance over the issue of interest rates. = *had a deciding confrontation.*

18 She ____**pped her hand**. = *gave a hint about her intentions.*

19 If you ____**ay your c**_____ **r**_____, you might succeed. = *make good use of your resources and opportunities*

20 Try to keep **a** _____ **face** during the negotiations = *not show your thoughts or feelings*

21 '**Blue** ___**ip**' means 'reputable and highly valued'.

Handout 6: Second Review Sheet

1 & 2   Of people who are secretive about their plans, we say that they like to play their _____s cl_____ to
         their ch_____. In other words, they never like to _____ their hands.

3   Let's stop hiding our thoughts. Let's lay all our c_____ ____ __ ____ t_____.

4   She didn't just win by a bit – she won by a lot! In other words, she won __ _____.

5   It's not going to happen. There's no chance. It's just not on the _____s.

6 & 7   We can afford to be tough in the negotiations tomorrow. We're holding all the _____. And if they
         give us any trouble, we've got one more _____ up our _____.

8 & 9   Sometimes you think she might be about to let you down, but she never does. She always c_____ up
         _____ in the e_____. In other words, you can rely on her when the _____s are down.

10   Mathematics is not my s_____ s_____.

11 & 12 He quit, gave up, _____ in his hand – i.e. f_____ – and walked away.

13   You can never tell how she will do. She's the _____ in the pack (or deck).

14   (Said just before a talk) If any of you have anything to contribute during the discussion, please do feel
         free to _____ in.

15   I suspect that the bidding process is unfair and that all of the bidders but one (the company owned by
         the president's brother) have the cards st_____ed against them.

16 & 17 Let's ___ the ante – you know, raise the st_____ – by demanding that all the bidders pay a non-
         refundable deposit.

18   The members of the board had a sh_____ with their chairman and told him that either he
         must resign or they would.

19   If you have an ace in the h_____, you have a hidden advantage.

20   Bl_____ _____ stocks and shares are the most reliable to buy, and are often the highest priced.

Handouts

Jigsaw texts

1 Great Britain has two kinds of navy, both of which were extremely large and important even as late as the 1950s. One kind is the Royal Navy, the oldest permanent part of the British armed forces (which is why it is still sometimes called the 'Senior Service'), and the other is the Merchant Navy, which consists of ships that carry commercial goods around the world. A hundred years ago, both navies were still the biggest of their kind in the world. Both are now much smaller than they once were, but it is easy to find evidence of their former great importance. For instance, a very high percentage of pubs have a sea-related name such as 'The Ship', 'The Anchor', 'The Trafalgar' (a famous sea battle), 'The Lord Nelson' (the British commander of the fleet at that battle), 'The Victory' (his ship), and so on. It is probably also true that the popularity of tattoos in Britain has something to do with its past as a seafaring nation.

continued ...

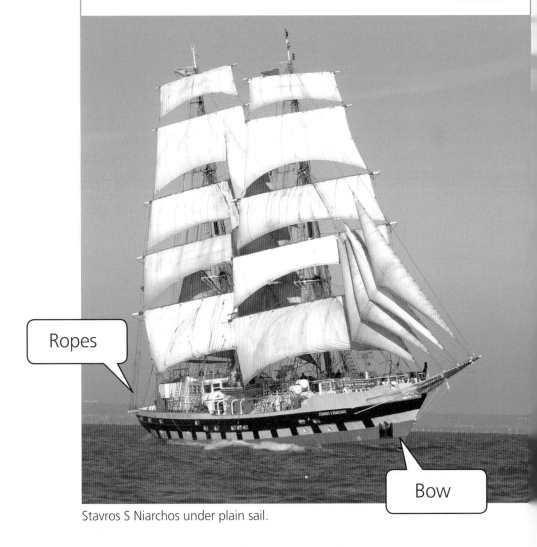

Stavros S Niarchos under plain sail.

Besides the Royal Navy and the Merchant Navy, Britain also had a huge fishing fleet and a considerable number of boats and ships engaged in carrying passengers. (Even today, many people and vehicles are carried to and from Britain in ferries, e.g. from the French port of Calais and the Dutch port of Hook of Holland). All in all, seafaring was a huge employer – especially of men and boys. (And this was true not only for towns and villages near the sea but also for ones in the interior of the country – although naturally not quite so much.) It was not at all uncommon for wives to see their husbands or parents their sons only once a year, or even less often than that. And of course in the old days, because seafaring was extremely dangerous, many wives became widows.

a) What are Britain's two navies called?

b) Do you think these navies were still the biggest of their kind in the world in the 1970s?

c) Why does this text mention pub names?

d) What about Britain's fishing fleet?

e) Are ferries still important, do you think?

f) Was it only men and boys living near the sea who got jobs on ships?

g) What did seafaring mean for family life?

2 In the last 500 years or so there were – as far as Europe was concerned – two main areas of piracy. One was the Mediterranean. The other was the Caribbean. In both cases, the 1600s were especially dangerous for seafarers. In the Mediterranean, Moorish pirates from North Africa captured ships (especially ones from Christian countries) and took passengers and crews into slavery by the thousands. (In the 1600s, Moorish pirates even captured people from villages in England, Ireland and Iceland!)

In and near the Caribbean, pirates attacked, in particular, Spanish ships carrying Aztec and Inca gold back to Spain. The exploits of some of these pirates – like Blackbeard and Henry Morgan – remain legendary. Sometimes they even conquered and pillaged whole cities. There were even a few famous and dangerous women pirate captains.

One reason the Caribbean was so lawless in the late 1500s and most of the 1600s is that Catholic Spain was long at war with Protestant countries such as England and the Netherlands. And so the English and the Dutch in some ways encouraged pirates (or 'freebooters') to attack Spanish shipping. And one reason why the Moors were able to carry out raids even against England itself was that during part of the 1600s the English were busy fighting each other; in the 1640s, there was a civil war. When stable government was restored in England in 1651 and when warfare between Protestant and Catholic countries became less constant, the Golden Age of piracy came to an end.

a) Where were the home ports of the Moorish pirates?
b) What did they generally do with the Christians that they captured?
c) What did the pirates of the Caribbean especially like to steal?
d) Why were the early 1600s the Golden Age of piracy?
e) Were all pirate captains men?
f) What were 'freebooters'?

3 Seafaring was an important source of work, but not just for sailors and fishermen. All those thousands of ships and boats needed to be built – and so thousands and thousands of people found work doing the construction.
Ships also needed to be supplied with sails and ropes and many other things – and that meant further work. And warships needed cannons and gunpowder. And sailors and passengers of all kinds needed food. In short, tens and tens of thousands of people all over Britain worked to make, equip and support the military, commercial and fishing fleets.
You don't see this so much today, at least not so widely. But the coast of Britain is to this day dotted with hundreds of marinas – places where recreational boats are kept for the hundreds of thousands of people who sail for fun. (Sailing is, after all, an Olympic sport – one in which the British do especially well.)
And there are a number of maritime (seafaring), museums. The most impressive is the National Maritime Museum in Greenwich, London. If you want to get a better idea of the hold that seafaring still has on the imagination of British people, try reading **Treasure Island** by Robert Louis Stevenson or any of the novels of C.S. Forester and Patrick O'Brian. British poetry and painting, too, are full of evidence of the importance of seafaring in British history and culture. Another bit of evidence of this – very important for anyone who wants to learn English well – is the dozens of idioms that come from seafaring; and now we are going to learn some!

a) Why does this text mention sails, ropes, cannons, food and so on?
b) About how many marinas are there and what are they?
c) Why does the text mention the Olympic sport of sailing?
d) Do few British people sail now?
e) What's in Greenwich?
f) Why does the text mention the novel **Treasure Island**?
g) What does the text say about idioms?

Idiom sentences

You'll <u>learn the ropes</u> in your first few weeks at work.

Who's going to <u>take the helm</u> after you retire?

She completed the project <u>under her own steam</u>.

He's in a bad mood. <u>Give him a wide berth</u>.

He turned white and then just <u>keeled over</u>. We picked him up and laid him on a sofa.

I don't think they need instructions about absolutely everything. <u>Give</u> them <u>a little</u> <u>leeway</u>.

We had workmen in the house last week. Talk about chaos! But we cleaned up after them and now <u>everything's shipshape</u>.

The method we've been following just doesn't work. Let's <u>try a different tack</u>.

He hasn't been <u>on an even keel</u> since the divorce. He even talked to me about maybe seeing a psychiatrist.

In the beginning, we had some problems, but once we solved them, It was all <u>plain sailing</u> from then on.

Look, you've only been working here for a week. I suggest you don't <u>rock the boat</u>, at least not until you know what's what.

<u>In the wake of</u> a bad earthquake there is almost always a desperate need for reconstruction.

Sea Fever (John Masefield)

I must (go) down / to the sea again, / to the lonely seas and the sky,

And all I ask / is a tall ship / and a star to steer her by,

And the wheel's kick / and the wind's song / and the white sails' shaking,

And a grey mist / on the sea's face / and a grey dawn breaking.

I must (go) down / to the seas again, / for the call of the running tide

Is a wild call / and a clear call / that may not be denied;

And all I ask / is a windy day / with the white clouds flying,

And the flung spray / and the blown spume, / and the sea-gulls crying.

I must (go) down / to the seas again / to the vagrant gypsy life,

To the gull's way / and the whale's way / where the wind's like a whetted knife;

And all I ask / is a merry yarn / from a laughing fellow-rover,

And quiet sleep / and a sweet dream / when the long trick's over.

Note

We have included 'go' in brackets, because it is included in some versions of the poem – Masefield himself changed his mind several times about it inclusion.

Handout

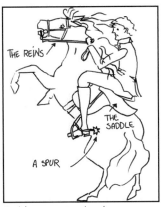

A rider on a rearing horse

Leading a horse by its bridle

A tethered horse

Horse Idioms and Sayings (To make the list easier, delete items from the end.)

1 She **keeps a tight rein on** her emotions.
a) keeps firm control over
b) enjoys

2 They experienced a night of **unbridled passion!**
a) controlled passion
b) uncontrolled passion

3 Their coach tried **to spur** his team **on** but they were too tired to try harder.
a) to insult his team
b) to cause his team to work harder and go faster

4 I'm almost **at the end of my tether**. If one more thing goes wrong, I'll go jump off a bridge.
a) at the end of what I have to do
b) at the limit of my mental strength and patience

5 **Give free rein to your** desires!
a) Release, set free
b) Redirect

6 This year's presidential election **was a one horse race**.
a) was won by one person, but only by one vote
b) wasn't a close contest at all

7 Higher pay can **be a spur to** better performance.
a) encourage
b) discourage

8 **Stop horsing around** and start working!
a) Stop moving around
b) Stop playing and being foolish

9 Will I come to your party? Of course I will! **Wild horses couldn't keep me away**. (a cliché)
a) Nothing could stop me from coming!
b) If you think the party will be too wild, I won't come.

10 Don't **put the cart before the horse**.
(a proverb; 'cart' UK 'wagon'US)
a) Don't do things in the wrong order.
b) Don't put something small before something big

11 **You can lead a horse to water but you can't make it drink**. (a proverb)
a) Horses are uncooperative.
b) You can give people advice but you can't usually make them follow it.

12 My parents live in **a one horse town.** There isn't even a cinema or a police station there.
a) a farming town
b) a small, quiet town where little ever happens

13 **Saddled with debt**, the company finally failed and went out of business.
a) – because it was carrying a heavy load of debt.
b) – because it had a few debts.

14 In times of **galloping inflation** don't put your money in a bank: spend it as fast as you can!
a) a very slow increase in prices
b) a very rapid increase in prices

15 After days of harmony and cooperation, disagreement **reared its ugly head**.
a) People still didn't disagree.
b) People began to disagree.

Note

For worksheets on other idiom sets, see www.helblinglanguages.com.

Handouts

Idioms Sheet. Which underlined expressions are *not* figurative?

Think of a synonym for each of the underlined idioms, or paraphrase it. If you don't understand one, skip it and go to the next. Then mark the idioms that are ***not*** figurative.

1 Don't be shy. If you want to get served, you'll just have to <u>elbow your way</u> to the bar.

2 He called her a liar, and then asked me to <u>back him up</u>. But my motto is 'Never get involved in an argument between a husband and wife'.

3 Teachers tell him what to do, but he won't <u>toe the line</u>. As a result, he has been expelled from three schools.

4 Nothing that comes from the government is free. The taxpayer always <u>foots the bill</u> in the end.

5 I can't tell you <u>off the top of my head</u>; I'll get back to you later.

6 She was so happy that everyone had remembered her birthday, <u>I didn't have the heart to tell her</u> that I knew her boss was going to fire her later that same day.

7 Let's not plan what to do. Let's just <u>play it by ear</u>.

8 That kid is <u>a pain in the neck</u> (or 'arse' ^{UK}/'ass'^{US}/'butt' ^{US}). I'd like to strangle him!

9 He said he would help us, but then he <u>got cold feet</u> when he realised how much work might be involved. Now we'll have to find someone else.

10 She <u>never put a foot wrong</u> all the time she worked for us. Never made a mistake. Never offended anyone.

11 He said 'Hi,' but she <u>gave him the cold shoulder</u>. You know, she hasn't forgiven him for how rude he was to her last week.

12 <u>Off-hand,</u> I don't know. Let's Google it and find out.

13 They asked their boss for more money, but he <u>rejected</u> their request <u>out of hand</u> – and I mean instantly, without a moment's thought

14 He'd make a terrible diplomat. He's always <u>putting his foot in his mouth</u>. Like the time he said how much he disliked Italian cooking just as his hostess was bringing the lasagne in from the kitchen.

15 He asked if he could borrow my car, and my driving licence too. <u>What a cheek!</u>

16 You know, if you <u>wear your heart on your sleeve</u> like that, she'll think you're acting like a silly love-struck teenager. Be more cool, a bit more reserved and adult.

17 They <u>tip-toed</u> out of the room so as not to wake the baby.

18 It's hard to learn a whole phone book <u>by heart</u>, but there are a few unusual people who can do it.

19 He's a gentleman <u>from head to toe</u>.

20 She's <u>head over heels in love</u>.

Little Red Riding Hood with body idioms
(based on the version of Charles Perrault, 1628-1703, at http://www.pitt.edu/~dash/type0333.html#perrault)

Once upon a time there lived in a certain village a little country girl, the prettiest creature who was ever seen. Her mother was exceedingly fond of her and her grandmother even more so. This good woman, her grandmother, had a little red riding hood made for the little girl – even though she didn't happen to have a pony. She wore the hood so often and it suited her so extremely well that everybody called her Little Red Riding Hood.

One day her mother, having made some cakes, said to her, "Go, my dear, and see how your grandmother is doing, for I hear she has been very ill. Take her a cake. Oh, and remember, don't **put your foot in it** – in your mouth, I mean – by telling her how old she looks or anything like that." Little Red Riding Hood set out immediately to go to her grandmother, who lived in another village. Because it was sunny, she didn't have her hood up. Just for fun, she carried the cake on the top of her head. As she was going through the wood, she met a wolf. Naturally, he wanted to eat her up right there and then, but he didn't dare because of some woodcutters working nearby in the forest. So he told her what beautiful hair she had, but asked her to take the cake **off the top of her head** so he could see it to better advantage.

She did so, saying, "You know, Mr Dog, I think on top of your head is a very handy place to keep a cake. It makes the cake so easy to reach." She also told him where she was going, for she was exceedingly friendly and chatty. The poor child did not know that it was dangerous to stay and talk to a wolf. In fact, she didn't even know what a wolf was!

"How far away does your grandma live?" asked the wolf, seemingly innocently. "In metres," he added.

The girl answered, "I can't tell you **off the top of my head**". That's not the kind of information I keep in mind all ready to remember. I'll have to ask Granny. But I can tell you her house is beyond that mill you see there, at the first house in the village."

The wolf couldn't believe his luck in finding such a friendly, chatty little girl. Some other girls he had met in the woods **had given him the cold shoulder**. And one particularly nasty little character had even zapped him in the face with pepper spray.

Anyway, as Little Red Riding Hood pointed in the direction of her granny's house, with her plump, juicy little pointing finger right by the tip of the wolf's damp, black nose, he thought for a second that he should just bite it off. But he quickly **got cold feet**, for he could hear two woodcutters moving around very nearby. "Well," said the wolf, "and I'll go and see her too. I'll go this way, and you go that, and we shall see who will be there first."

"What fun!" said Little Red Riding Hood.

The wolf ran as fast as he could, taking the shortest path. He ran so fast, in fact, that he tripped once over a root and fell **head over heels** into a mud puddle. Meanwhile, the little girl took a roundabout way which involved crossing a stream on a log. As she made her way across it, she was careful not to **put a foot wrong**, as she didn't want to fall in and get all wet and muddy. When she had reached the other side, she decided to pick a bouquet of wild flowers for her granny. And when she had finished, she sat down and took out the harmonica she always carried in her coat pocket and played her own favourite tune. She **played it by ear** since she had never learned how to read music. Then, after a while, she put her harmonica away and continued on her way.

As for the wolf, it was not long before he arrived at the old woman's house. But when he got there, he realised that he didn't have a plan. He wondered for a split second what to do and in what order, but then thought, "I'll just **play it by ear**. I'll see what 'granny' does and react accordingly." So he knocked at the door tap, tap, tap.

"Who's there?" came the old lady's voice.

"Your grandchild, Little Red Riding Hood. I've brought you a cake and a little pot of butter sent you by Mother," replied the wolf, imitating the little girl quite well considering he was a wolf.

The good grandmother called out, "Come in. I'm in bed and don't want to get up." When the wolf entered, he saw the old woman in bed and right beside her, on top of a stool, was a plate with two shoulders of roast lamb on it. He thought he would eat them first because she wasn't very big, and looked tough and thin at that. Still pretending to be Little Red Riding Hood, he asked as politely as he could if he might snack on a shoulder of lamb. But the grandmother **gave him the cold shoulder** since she wasn't completely sure this visitor was Little Red Riding Hood after all, and she didn't want to give away the much tastier warm shoulder of lamb.

Well, the wolf ate the shoulder so fast that the old woman was now even more suspicious. She decided to test him: "Sing a song for me. One with a lively, cheerful tune!" she said. (You remember of course that Little Red Riding Hood was **very** musical.) So the wolf sang, but it was horrible. Unlike the little girl, he **couldn't carry a tune in a basket**, let alone carry one on his hoarse, wolfy voice. After only six notes he could see that the old lady knew he wasn't her grand-daughter, so he decided to eat her before she tried to escape. But he had **got cold feet** standing on Granny's cold stone floor. Quickly, he put on her slippers so that at least half of his feet were warm.

"How many calories do you contain?" he asked her. Although shocked by his impertinence, Granny answered rather coolly, "I don't know **offhand**. I think I have the number written down somewhere."

This answer didn't please the wolf, so he jumped her anyway and devoured her **from head to toe**. One of her hairpins got stuck in his throat, though, so he had to **put his foot in his mouth**, his right front foot to be exact, in order to get it out.

Then the wolf got into the grandmother's nightie and got into bed to await Little Red Riding Hood. She, meanwhile, had met one of the woodcutters. He was reading a book during his lunch break.

"What are you reading?" Red asked.

"Poems by Shakespeare," he answered. "I've just learned one **by heart**." And to prove it, he closed his book and recited it to her most beautifully.

"He must be very romantic by nature," she thought, for sewed onto one of his sleeves there was a heart cut out of blood-red woollen cloth. "Do you always **wear your heart on your sleeve** like that?" she asked.

"Yes," he said. "I'm **head over heels** in love with someone, and I can't keep it a secret. Everyone can see it. I guess I'm just a romantic **from head to toe**. But I have another heart; I'll give it to you."

"No, thank you," said Little Red Riding Hood. "I'm sure my mother wouldn't let me wear it. Anyway, I'm not in love." And with that she continued on her way, but a little bit ashamed of herself for rejecting the romantic

woodcutter's offer **out of hand**. That hadn't been very polite of her, she thought. She decided that if she saw him again she would apologise and accept his spare red woollen heart.

But now she came to her gran's little cottage. Wanting to surprise her dear, sweet gran, she approached the door **on tiptoe** and then tapped on it very, very softly: tap, tap, tap.

"Who's there?" called out the wolf, who had forgotten to try to imitate the old woman.

Little Red Riding Hood, hearing the hoarse voice of the wolf, was at first afraid, but then thought maybe her grandmother had a cold or something. So she replied, "It's me, Gran, and I have a little surprise for you from mother!"

The wolf called out to her, softening his voice as much as he could, "Come in, come in! Oh, do come in!" and hiding under the bedclothes, he watched her come in with the cake once more on top of her head. "Oh!" he said, "How sweet you both are, you and your mum. Put the cake on this little table and come, get into bed with me to keep me warm."

Little Red Riding Hood did as she was told, and got into bed. But she was astonished to see how different her grandmother looked from how she used to, and said,

"Grandmother, what big arms you have!"

"All the better to hug you with, my dear."

"Grandmother, what a lot of hairy legs you have!"

"All the better to run with, my child."

"Grandmother, what big ears you have!"

"All the better to hear you with, my child."

"Grandmother, what big eyes you have!"

"All the better to see you with, my child."

"Grandmother, what big teeth you've got!"

"All the better to **eat** you with!"

And saying these words, the wicked wolf fell upon Little Red Riding Hood, and ate her up.

Moral: children – most especially attractive, well-bred young ladies – should never talk to strangers, for if they should do so, they may well provide dinner for a wolf. I say 'wolf', but there are various kinds of wolves. There are also those who are charming, quiet, polite, unassuming, complacent and sweet, who pursue young women at home and in the streets. And unfortunately, it is these gentle wolves who are the most dangerous ones of all.

3.9 Handouts

Idioms Review Sheet

1   Teachers tell him what to do, but he won't **t___ the l_____** . As a result, he has been expelled from three schools.

2   Nothing that comes from the government is free. The taxpayer always **f_____ the __ill** in the end.

3   She's a lady from **head to _____**.

4   It's hard to learn a whole phone book **__y h_____**, but there are a few unusual people who can do it.

5   I can't tell you **off the t____ of my h_____**; I'll get back to you later.

6   She tip-_____ out of the room so as not to wake the baby.

7   Let's not plan what to do. Let's just **pl____ it by e_____.**

8   That kid is **a p_____ in the _____**. I'd like to strangle him!

9   They're **head over _____ in love** with each other.

10 He said he would help us, but then **got co_____ f_____** when he realised how much work might be involved. Now we'll have to find someone else.

11 She **never p____ a f_____ _____ng** all the time she worked for us. Never made a mistake. Never offended anyone.

12 He said 'Hi', but she gave him **the co____ sh_____**. You know, she hasn't forgiven him for how rude he was to her last week.

13 **Offh_____**, I don't know. Let's Google it and find out.

14 Don't be shy. If you want to get served at this pub, you'll just have to **___bow your w____** to the bar.

15 They asked their boss for more money, but he **rejected** their request **o____ of h_____** – and I mean instantly, without a moment's thought.

16 He'd make a terrible diplomat. He's always **p_____ing his f_____ in his m_____**. Like the time he said how much he disliked Italian cooking just as his hostess was bringing the lasagne in from the kitchen.

17 She was so happy that everyone had remembered her birthday, I **didn't have the h_____ to t____l her** that I knew her boss was going to fire her later that same day.

18 He asked if he could borrow my car and my driving licence too. **What a ch_____!**

19 You know, if you **w_____ your h_____ on your sl_____** like that, he'll think you're acting like a silly love-struck teenager. Be more cool, a woman of mystery!

20 He called her a liar, and then asked me to **b_____** him **u____**. But my motto is 'Never get involved in an argument between a wife and a husband'.

138   © Helbling Languages. Please photocopy this page for use in class

3.10

Worksheet

An idiom typically evokes a scene that is part of a larger scenario. For example, a debate between two politicians can be described as if it were a boxing match. English has more than a dozen idioms that are derived from boxing, but the particular idiom you choose from the whole set will highlight a specific stage of the fight/debate and a particular intensity of conflict. With this in mind, can you put the following expressions into the right blanks in the text below?

lower his guard	*in a tight corner*	*on the ropes*
the gloves are off	*not pull their punches*	*throw in the towel*
take it on the chin	*flex their muscles*	
out for the count	*stick his neck out*	

Before a debate begins two opposing politicians may metaphorically (1)_____ to frighten the opponent; during the debate one of them may carelessly (2)_____ or bravely (3)_____ and perhaps (4)_____; if the debate gets more intense the two opponents will (5) _____; and after a while either of them may (6)_____ , that is, admit defeat rather than risk getting hit hard and then going (7)_____.

If you feel the debate is getting out of hand and the two parties are really wanting to hurt each other, then you can say that (8)_____.

(9) Which of the following two idioms expresses most strongly that one of the politicians is losing the debate: "He's in a tight corner now", or "He's on the ropes now"?

Handouts

Idioms and their Meanings

Which six meanings are not matched to the right idioms? Which idioms **should** they go with instead?

1	*Oh, <u>come off it</u>!*	= 'Stop being so ridiculously self-important; stop thinking you can fool me.'
2	*He really <u>took it on the chin</u>.*	= coped with a painful experience of some kind
3	*You really <u>blew it</u> that time* (i.e. blew it away)	= 'You're welcome'
4	*<u>Shut it</u>!*	= 'Stop talking!'
5	*<u>Drop it</u>!*	= 'Stop fighting' or 'Separate and go away'
6	*<u>Don't mention it</u>.*	= made a big mistake
7	*<u>Cut it out</u>!*	= 'Stop doing what you're doing!'
8	*<u>Break it up</u>! =*	= 'Stop talking about that topic!"
9	*I'm going to <u>lose it</u> if he's late again.*	= 'Go away!'
10	*Welcome! I'm glad you could <u>make it</u>.*	= come
11	*<u>Beat it</u>!*	= get upset
12	*You really <u>dropped me in it</u> when you told the hostess I hadn't really wanted to come.*	= put me in an embarrassing situation
13	*Good work! <u>Keep it up</u>!*	= 'Continue with what you're doing'
14	*I really <u>put my foot in it</u>.*	= said something that was very embarrassing for sb
15	*I just don't <u>get it</u>.*	= understand

What *it* originally stood for

	matches sentence number
a) (My) temper, self-control	....
b) the trip	....
c) a high place like a stage or speaker's platform	....
d) the road (i.e. with your feet)	....
e) the shit	....
f) this gathering of people; this close contact between two people	....
g) what you are doing (as if it was something like the bad part of an apple)	....
h) a punch	....
i) the subject of the conversation up to this point	....
j) what you say I did for you	....
k) the point (of what someone has said or done), the basic meaning or reason	....
l) your mouth	....
m) my mouth	....
n) the effort	....
o) a golden opportunity, a good situation in life	....

Note
- ***Come off it!*** is something you might say to someone who you think is saying something they don't really believe, like an actor playing a ridiculous part.
- ***Break it up!*** is something policemen might say to a crowd of spectators at a crime scene in order to make them separate and go away; or a referee might say this to two boxers who are holding onto each other so they can't actually box.
- In modern British English a predictable noun may be replaced not by ***it*** but by 'the proverbial' – ***You really dropped me in <u>the proverbial</u>*** (= shit)***.*** This seems especially common when the speaker wants to be euphemistic. Sometimes ***the proverbial*** replaces a whole phrase – e.g. ***I'm up the proverbial*** (= shit creek) ***without a paddle.***

Additional idioms of this kind
- ***Pull it off*** = succeed despite difficulty or long odds. ***It*** may refer to a ring placed on a pole near a merry-go-round; riders on the merry-go-round stretched out their arms to try to get the ring. If they managed to pull it off, they won a prize.
- ***Make it up to sb*** = compensate sb. ***It*** means some kind of shortfall. ***Up*** probably has the meaning seen in ***fill up***, i.e. completely.
- ***Be past it*** = be past the prime of your life, be too old to cope.
- ***Stick it to sb*** = make someone really suffer, show no mercy. ***It*** refers to a knife.

Alternatives for extension

1	She passed out but then quickly came to./	fingers
2	It was rather heated debate but she held her own./	resources
3	She lives on her own./	herself
4	Take five./	from the scene of the crime, from the police
5	Give me five./	minutes of rest
6	Great victory! We really put the boot in./	ground
7	He got away / with murder.	[their] ribs

Notes
- come to = 'regain consciousness'. In the 19th century people sometimes still said come to yourself. This is just one example of people talking about being in an abnormal state of mind as 'not being in one's normal place'; e.g., be beside yourself [with anger] = be utterly furious; be out to lunch, be with the fairies, be in outer space = be out of touch with reality.
- Hold your own ground originally meant 'Don't retreat; don't give up any of your territory to the enemy.'
- on your own can also include the meaning 'alone'.
- Take five. Said to solders as a signal to rest, e.g., during a difficult march.
- Give me five! means 'Let's slap hands in greeting or to show mutual respect'.
- Put the boot in. The full form seems to be Put the boot into their ribs. = kick[ed] them hard.

Idioms grouped by source domain

The following idioms have been found to lend themselves well to this procedure. These are **all** expressions that are signalled in **The Collins Cobuild Dictionary of Idioms** as 'frequently used'.

From card games: *Call sb's bluff, Above board, Pass the buck, Get s'thing off your chest, Get a raw deal, Follow suit, Not miss a trick, Force sb's hand, The luck of the draw.* (See also 3.6)

From gambling games generally: *Back to square one, Turn the tables on sb, Break the bank, Draw a blank, Hit the jackpot, play Russian roulette, There's the rub, Get an even break, Cash in your chips, When the chips are down, The dice are loaded against me, Lose your shirt.*

From horse racing: *They're neck and neck, Hedge your bets, Across the board, Go for broke, Too close to call, Win hands down, Be a dark horse (in a contest), Pay over the odds (for s'thing), Pip sb at the post, Be in the running, Horses for courses.* (See also 3.8.)

From ball games and track sports: *The ball's in your court, (Score) an own goal, Be off base, Play into sb's hands, Par for the course, Toe the line, Jump the gun, Be quick off the mark, Hit sb for six, Have the inside track (on sb), Start from scratch, Blow the whistle on sb, A level playing field, Below par, Sb's track record, Three strikes and you're out.*

From hunting and shooting contests: *It's open season on sb, Set your sights on s'thing, Give s'thing your best shot, It's in the bag, Be a sitting duck, A long shot, Be/shoot wide of the mark, A red herring, (Stand by sb) through thick and thin, Run riot, Hit and miss, A mixed bag.*

From boxing and the martial arts: *Throw sb off balance, Take it on the chin, Be in a tight corner, Go the full distance, At the drop of a hat, Lower your guard, Head to head, No holds barred, Be on the ropes, Flex your muscles, Stick your neck out, Not pull your punches, Not come up to scratch, Throw in the towel (or sponge), Throw down the gauntlet.* (See also 3.10.)

From warfare: *Be up in arms about s'thing, Be in the front line, A baptism of fire, Fight a rearguard action, A last-ditch attempt, Stick to your guns, Steal a march on sb, Be the standard bearer, Gain ground (on sb), Stand shoulder to shoulder (with sb), Break ranks, Happen on sb's watch, Catch sb off guard, Be at loggerheads with sb, Burn your bridges (or boats).*

From seafaring: *Take s'thing on board, Have a close call, Be a loose cannon, Steer clear of sb, Stay the course, (Pass an exam) with flying colours, Be dead in the water, Clear the deck(s) (for action), Be in the doldrums, Be on an even keel, Be left high and dry, Break the ice, Be a leading light, Be at sea, A shot across sb's bows, Be just the tip of the iceberg, Be at a loose end (as with a flapping sail) Show your true colours.* (See also 3.7.)

From horse-riding: *Give sb a leg up, Ride roughshod over sb, Ride high (in the saddle), Put sb through their paces.* (See also 3.8.)

From other means of transport, and roads: *Get into gear, (Live life) in the fast lane, Get the green light (to do s'thing), Middle-of-the-road (tastes), Go into overdrive, Be on automatic pilot, Be in the driving seat, Be in a rut, Take a back seat (to sb), Be on the skids, Make the grade, Hit the buffers, Be a back-seat driver, Come to a crossroads (in life).*

From the animal world: *Go belly-up, A bone of contention, A carrot-and-stick method, Ruffle sb's feathers, A feeding frenzy, Spread your wings, Bite the hand that feeds you, Bury your head in the sand, Call sb to heel, Go for the jugular, Be out on a limb, Poke your nose into s'thing, Be (high/low) in the pecking order, See red, Rule the roost, Come out of your shell, Have a sting in the tail, Be at each other's throats, Get wind of s'thing, Take sb under your wing, Clip sb's wings, Rub sb's nose in it, Have no strings attached, Those chickens will come home to roost, Lick your wounds, Raise sb's hackles, Be off the hook.*

From entertainment: *Take centre stage, Perform a (delicate) balancing act, The curtain comes down, A one-man band, Set the stage for s'thing, (Act/See) behind the scenes, Pull the strings, The villain of the piece, Jump onto the bandwagon, Strike a chord with sb, Play second fiddle to sb, Give sb/s'thing the thumbs up, Face the music, Pull out all the stops, Call the tune, Pull s'thing out of the hat, Change your tune, Walk a tightrope, In the limelight.*

From food and drink: *Small beer, Tighten your belt, Put s'thing on the back burner, Be past one's sell-by date, The flavour of the month, Live from hand to mouth, Go the whole hog, Live high on the hog, Put s'thing on ice, The icing on the cake, A piece of cake, Get handed* s'thing on a plate, Have enough on your plate, A hot potato, Take pot luck, Take s'thing with a pinch of salt, On tap, Call time on s'thing.

From commerce and accounting: *Go under the hammer^{UK} / Be on the (auction) block^{US}, Pay dividends, Make ends meet, Hang in the balance, Ring hollow, Be given a new lease of life, The bottom line, Make a pitch for s'thing, Be worth your salt, Wipe the slate clean, Keep tabs on sb, Tip the balance, Be back in business.*

From jurisdiction and punishment: *Be caught red-handed, Be brought to book, The jury is still out (on that matter), Sign sb's death warrant, Seal sb's fate, Turn up the heat on sb, Tighten the screw on sb, Rub salt into sb's wounds, A ball and chain, Get the chop, Get egg on your face, Run the gauntlet, Rap sb on the knuckles, Give sb/Get short shrift.*

From gardening and agriculture: *Prepare the ground for, Sow the seeds (of a problem), Take root, Nip s'thing in the bud, Bear fruit, Have a field day, Be cut and dried, Be grist for the mill, A thorny problem, The root of the problem.*

From sewing, handicraft and manufacturing: *Lose your thread, Be at a loose end, Be made to measure, Be tailor-made, Chop and change, Go back to the drawing board, Take the edge off s'thing, Go against the grain, Break the mould, A rule of thumb, Be a dyed-in-the-wool s'thing, Knock s'thing into shape.*

From mechanics and technology: *Recharge your batteries, At the touch of a button, Be firing on all cylinders, Put a damper on s'thing, Blow up in your face, Get a fix on s'thing/sb, Be in the groove, Run-of-the-mill, The penny's dropped, Pull the plug on s'thing, Prime the pump, Throw a spanner^{UK}/monkey-wrench^{US} in the works, Be in full swing, Be on the same wave-length.*

More Idioms, for Advanced Learners

The following idioms (which belong to a slightly lower frequency band than the ones in the main list of Idioms Grouped by Source Domain) could be additional suitable targets for sorting by source domain:

make a pitch for something (hint: market)

jump through hoops (hint: circus)

juggle a lot of balls in the air (hint: circus)

pass the baton (hint: track sports)

play it by ear (hint: music)

pass the hat around (hint: street or market performers)

play to the gallery (hint: theatre)

be waiting in the wings (hint: theatre)

turn tail (hint: animal)

live off the backs of others (hint: birds)

foul your own nest (hint: birds)

the fur is flying (hint: cats)

keep a tight leash on someone (hint: dogs)

pat on the back (hint: dogs, horses)

be put off the scent (hint: dogs)

bark up the wrong tree (hint: dogs)

be put out to grass/pasture (hint: horses)

work in harness (hint: horses)

put out feelers (hint: snails, insects)

overstep the mark (track sports)

walk the plank (hint: seafaring; pirates).

shove your oar in (hint: rowing)

rub someone (up) the wrong way (hint: dogs, horses)

be ahead of the pack (hint: wolves)

move the goalposts (hint: ball games)

be sent from pillar to post (hint: racing);

cover all the bases (hint: baseball, cricket)

roll with the punches (hint: boxing)

argue the toss (hint: ball games)

be in pole position (hint: car racing).

Handout

It has become a widely accepted idea in western culture that instead of bottling up our emotions we should air them now and then. For example, if we're frustrated, ventilating our feelings, or blowing off steam, may help us to avoid any sudden explosion of emotion.

But this can generate a serious problem. As it happens, releasing, or ventilating, anger is a particularly bad way to cool down. An outburst of rage typically pumps us up, making us feel ***more*** angry, not less. And if we reach boiling point and blow up at someone who has provoked our anger, our rage reaches a yet higher peak, and our angry mood is prolonged. Also, we may well erupt in rage even at innocent bystanders – and, worse, our nearest and dearest – and continue to fume much longer after our outburst than if we had not unleashed our rage.

A far more effective way of managing anger is to take advantage of our human ability to 'step back' mentally, and observe our own feelings and behaviour. This naturally results in us simmering down, without any further effort on our part. It also gives us the opportunity to look at the issue from the other person's viewpoint, so that we can constructively seek a solution with them.

Based on Goleman (2006) and S. N. Goenka, Vipassana, December 2007

Figurative expressions of anger

There's no reason to snap at me like that!
You're driving me nuts.
Don't bite my head off!
Her attitude had him climbing the walls.
Simmer down!
That kind of remark just adds fuel to the fire.
He went berserk when I told him.
He was breathing fire.
He looks hot under the collar.

She got all steamed up.
I'm reaching my boiling point.
She blew up at me.
He's blowing off steam.
Anger welled up inside him.
I was fuming with anger.
I'm mad at him.
Those were inflammatory remarks.
Don't rub him up the wrong way.

Worksheet

Write each of the following words under the appropriate picture. Begin with the four verbs in capital letters. There are more writing lines than you need, and some nouns can follow more than one verb.

COMMIT	CONDUCT	PERFORM	CAUSE
adultery	*arson*	*a burglary*	*a ceremony*
a crime	*a dance*	*a miracle*	*a murder*
a play	*a robbery*	*destruction*	*a solo*
a song	*a study*	*a survey*	*an assault*
devastation	*an experiment*	*an inquiry*	*an inspection*
an interview	*an investigation*	*an offence*	*an atrocity*
damage	*havoc*	*research*	*suicide*

1 *Eat well to be healthy.*

2 *I stopped to tie my shoes.*

3 *You know, I forgot about meeting her until I saw that photo of her and me together.*

4 *I avoided contributing by saying I needed the money for a taxi.*

5 *I forgot to phone.*

6 *I stopped smoking last year.*

7 *I refused to pay.*

8 *He threatened to come.*

9 *I regret leaving.*

10 *I promised to do it.*

11 *I agreed to do it.*

12 *I couldn't afford to go.*

13 *I'm considering leaving.*

14 *I was forced to come.*

15 *I miss seeing her.*

Worksheets:
'Which is the catchiest?'

Instructions for all levels:

First, fill in the missing letter(s) for each option. Then, cross out the word which is less catchy. Finally, highlight the letter for the sound that is repeated. For example:

1   Some people dislike | _oy / _uy | bands.
2   Some people dislike | boy / guy | bands.
3   Some people dislike | boy / ~~guy~~ | bands.
4   Some people dislike | (boy / ~~guy~~ | bands.

Note: Although all the word combinations are possible, the ones which provide sound repetition are particularly natural.

Pre-intermediate

1   Keep | __pproaching! / __oming! |

2   He drank the poison and just | _ropped / _ell | dead.

3   The | __lackest / __arkest | hour is just before the dawn.

4 | __ orbidden / __aboo | fruit is the sweetest.

5   Welcome! We like to see a | __ew / __resh | | __erson / __ace | around here now and then.

6   Who's the | __oss / __ead | of the house? The mother? The father? Both?

7   I've got a | __trange / __unny | feeling I've seen this film before.

8   What a sweet child. She's as good as | __ilver / __old |.

9   When I'm old I don't just want to sit around and watch the | __lants / __rass | grow. I want to do things … have fun!

10 She lost her job. Then, to make | __hings / __atters | worse, she fell ill.

11 In her new dress she looked as | __retty / __ovely | as a picture.

12 When the cat's away the mice will | __ave a good time / __lay |.

13 He went from hero to | __othing / __ero | in one week.

14 The | __arger / __igger | the better.

15 Say, you look in | __ine / __reat | shape!

16 These two boxers hate each other so this is going to be a fight to the | __inish / __nd |.

17 In this office we're like one big, | __lad / __appy | family.

18 I can't tell you. It's a deep | __lack / __ark | secret.

19 Here he comes, | __oney / __ash | in hand, ready to pay.

20 It's late. I'm going to | __eave / __ead | for home.

Intermediate

1 Since his promotion, he's got too big for his | __hoes / __oots | .

2 Finally, that killer is | in __rison / behind __ars |

3 When you're in the middle of a car crash, sometimes you see everything happen in slow | __ovement / __otion |.

4 I just can't | __ear / __arry | this heavy burden of responsibility any longer.

5 Her outfits are always so well colour | __o-ordinated / __atched | .

6 Sometimes, say psychologists, you have to be | __asty / __ruel | to be kind.

7 That bullet came too | __lose / __ear | for comfort.

8 He's so vain. He thinks he's God's | __resent / __ift | (to women).

9 Helping her across the street was my good | __ct / __eed | for the day.

10 Look before you | __ump / __eap | .

11 The lesson was so deadly | __ull / __oring | I slept through most of it.

12 He's the government's expert on foreign | a__airs / re__ations | .

13 Oh, I'm | __ell / __ery | aware of how wonderful you are. You don't need to tell me.

14 He's very imaginative but he's not very good with facts and | __igures / __umbers | .

15 You'd better get a new car. This one is on its last | __eet / __egs | .

16 His plan had a fatal | __mperfection / __law | and disaster was the result.

17 She fell head over | __eet / __eels | in love with him.

18 Love her or | __ate / __oathe | her, you have to admit she's good at her job.

19 When you're in the middle of a car crash, sometimes you see everything happen in slow | __ovement / __otion |.

20 All these cares and | __oncerns / __orries | are driving me crazy. I never wanted to be a mother!

21 I never thought a plane that big could | __et / __ise | off the ground.

22 She had such | __ntense / __igh | hopes for her children but they've all turned out to be losers.

23 Who was the | __tarring / __eading | | l__dy / __ctress | in that film?

24 You never know when disaster may | __appen / __trike |.

25 She didn't like what you said to her. If looks could | __ill / __urder | , you'd be dead now.

26 That part of the city is a no go | ar__a / z__ne |

27 She lost her job. Then, to make | __hings / __atters | worse, she fell ill.

28 She changed jobs with | __ixed / __onfused | emotions; part of her was sorry, part of her was glad.

29 He spends | __ext / __lose | to nothing on clothes. That's why he has no job and no girlfriend.

30 'He was born with a | __olden / __ilver | spoon in his mouth' is a way of saying that someone grew up in a rich family and had a very easy life right from the start. (One critic of George Bush II said he was born with a silver foot in his mouth.)

31 Someone born into a poor family has to start from [__ero / __cratch] if they want to get rich.

32 There were signs of a [__truggle / __ight] at the scene of the crime.

33 Well, you've broken it. I hope you're [__lad / __appy].

34 Don't complain. He won fair and [hon__st / squ__re].

35 He never [li__ted / rai__ed] a finger to help her when she was in trouble.

36 Well. That's another day done. It's time to [sh__t / cl__se] up shop and go home.

37 In general, the job of UN soldiers is to [m___ntain / k___p] the peace.

Upper intermediate

1 Beauty is in the eye of the [__eholder / __iewer].

2 When their business failed, they lost all their worldly [__ealth / __ssets].

3 We're so grateful. What you did for us was [o__er / a___ove] and beyond the call of duty.

4 Elizabeth I of England seemed the perfect queen in both word and [dee__ / actio__].

5 Nurse, hurry! The patient in bed four has [___anged / taken a t__rn] for the worse.

6 Such behaviour is beyond the [__ounds / __imits] of acceptability.

7 We had a whole [__rowd / __ost] of problems.

8 Not everyone has the courage of their [__eliefs / __onvictions].

9 I think we've finally broken the [__egs / __ack] of this problem.

10 Most magicians can do some kind of [d__sappearing / v__nishing] act.

11 Come to your party? You bet your [__hoes / __oots] I will!

12 This is the boss's [__et / __avourite] project, so don't make any mistakes.

13 Since 2008, there's been a [__eneral / __lanket] ban on smoking in pubs in England.

14 There's a [__oophole / __ap] in the law that may allow us to avoid paying half our taxes this year.

15 Their house burned down, but there was one [_it / __rumb] of comfort. It was insured.

16 That's against our [code of __onduct / rules of __ehaviour].

17 We're starting to [__in against / __ain ground on] the opposition. We should catch up soon.

18 You'd better get a new car. This one is on its last [__eet / __egs].

19 Low [__ltitude / __ying] land can get flooded.

20 That lazy, no-good child has made her life a [__ragedy / __isery].

21 All Chinese are good cooks?! That's a rather [__eneral / __weeping] statement!

22 If you have a question about electrical systems, ask my dad. He really knows his [c__rrots / o__ions].

23 Not all is gold that [__hines / __listens].

24 During their divorce, the main [fo__us / bo__e] of contention between them was who was going to get their beach house.

25 This contract isn't worth the paper it's `__ritten / __rinted` on.

26 Women have a lot more `__urchasing / __uying` power than they did a hundred years ago.

27 Somehow, his explanation doesn't `__ound / __ing` true.

28 The report on the disaster is pretty `sh__cking / gr__m` reading, but as it's your job to know the facts, here it is.

29 Their business has suffered a serious `__eversal / __etback`. They may lose all their money.

30 Look at her dance! That's `__iterature / __oetry` in motion!

31 Running a marathon is a real test of `__tamina / __ndurance`.

32 Most good crime novels have a twist in the `__nding / __ail`.

33 When that business failed, I lost all my worldly `__ealth / __iches`.

34 Naming and `d__sgracing / sh__ming` vandals and litterers in the local paper won't work if they don't care what anyone thinks of them.

35 We can't cancel our reservation at this late `__ay / __ate`.

36 And so, ladies and gentlemen, the `__orthy / __eserving` winner is … the lady in seat 24, who got all answers correct!

37 Construction is finished – on time and well `__nside / __ithin` budget.

38 It's a top `n__tch / qu__lity` product.

39 She was `p__lling out / t__aring` her hair in desperation.

40 We'd better call a `st__p / h__lt` to the experiment. People are starting to get sick.

41 What happened last night just goes to `sho__ / prov__` that you can't drink two bottles of wine and still function.

42 She succeeded in her last `br__ath / g__sp` attempt.

Advanced

1 With this car, you get more | __ang for your buck / results for your __ollar |.

2 She's been | __age-struck / attracted by the __eatre | ever since she was a little girl.

3 He's lucky. He's got brains and | _uscles / _rawn |.

4 Here's your car, restored to its former | c__ndition / gl___y |. That will be £1,400, please.

5 You can see him near the temple every day with his begging | __owl / __late |, waiting for passers-by to give him money.

6 I lost a lot at the casino. Oh well, that's the way the | __ookie / __iscuit | crumbles.

7 Were you born in a | __table / __arn |? Close the door!

8 The fighting was | __lose up / at close __uarters |, with swords and fists.

9 Every | __og / __at | has its day. And someday I'll have mine! Just you wait and see.

10 I think we'll have to look farther | a__ay / a__ield | if we want to find the right person for this job. There won't be anyone with the right qualifications around here, I don't think.

11 Around other children, she's a bit of a little miss bossy | __oots / __hoes |; it's been hard for her to make friends.

12 Don't | __ause me any __rouble / __ive me any __rief | over this, will you. We're behind schedule as it is.

13 Who's the head | __oncho / __erson | around here?

14 An explorer has to have a good memory for the | __ie / __ontours | of the land.

15 The idea of going there on holiday lost its | __hine / __ustre | when I heard that they were in the middle of a civil war,

16 This make of car is much | __aligned / __riticised |. But we've got one and we're very happy with it.

17 It's of | __aramount / __reat | importance that you be at that meeting tomorrow.

18 Such behaviour is beyond the | __ounds / __imits | of acceptability.

19 For the modern academic, the | __ule / __ame | of the game is publish or | __ie / __erish |.

20 She was | __illoried / sharply __riticised | in the press for abandoning her children.

21 Rumours are | __verywhere / __ife | that you've secretly remarried. So?

22 Having lost all his money, he's living in rather | __traitened /__ mpoverished | circumstances.

23 A certain | __omebody / __ou-know-who | told me you were looking for me. So here I am.

24 I have a | __ittle / __neaking | suspicion that you're not telling me the whole truth.

25 Some people like shows that | a__ack / a__ault | the senses. But loud music and bright lights are not for me.

26 You can have the best | __ntentions / __ill | in the world but still you're sometimes going to make mistakes and disappoint people.

27 Get every last credit card you have. Let's go on the mother of all shopping | __inges / __prees |!

28 She's so quiet and shy she wouldn't say boo to a | d___ck / g____se |.

29 Rupert Murdoch is a famous media | __ycoon / __oghul |.

3.17

Chunks to sort

Pre-intermediate and/or intermediate

1 He has a <u>beer belly</u>.
2 They <u>made a mistake</u>.
3 The storm <u>did</u> a lot of <u>damage</u>.
4 Let's <u>bake a cake</u>.
5 <u>The more the merrier</u>.
6 They <u>took a trip</u> around the world.
7 Airport book shops mainly have <u>best-sellers.</u>
8 She just got back from <u>a world tour.</u>
9 Let's not wait. <u>It's now or never.</u>
10 <u>Forgive and forget</u>.
11 You <u>look as pretty as a picture</u>.
12 It rained all day, <u>on and on</u>.
13 Have you got good or bad <u>eyesight?</u>
14 <u>What a mess</u> you've <u>made!</u>
15 It's <u>up to you</u>. (= the decision is yours)
16 That happens <u>from time to time</u>.
17 <u>Keep it clean</u>.
18 <u>Tell the truth</u>.
19 Did you <u>find the time</u> to phone her?
20 Is that <u>the right size</u> for you?
21 Take a <u>good look</u>.
22 Do it <u>as fast as you can</u>.
23 <u>How about</u> going to the beach?
24 Do I hear <u>wedding bells?</u>
25 There's <u>bad blood between</u> them.
26 We've never <u>spoken face to face</u>.
27 We don't give credit. It's <u>pay as you go</u>.
28 Let's do it right now. <u>The time is right.</u>
29 Things are getting better, <u>little by little</u>.
30 <u>The bigger the better</u>.
31 <u>I see what you mean</u>.
32 She visits her family <u>on a daily basis</u>.
33 Let's give our first speaker <u>a warm welcome</u>!
34 Yes, that's <u>an important point</u>. Thank you for mentioning it.
35 He likes being <u>a house husband</u>.

Upper intermediate and/or advanced

1 It's a <u>make or break</u> situation.
2 We're <u>spoilt for choice</u>.^{UK}
3 <u>The less said the better</u>.
4 <u>Speak of the devil</u>!
5 What's <u>the age range</u> of the kids at your school?
6 He fell out of the boat and <u>sank like a stone</u>.
7 She's <u>an asylum seeker</u>.
8 He's evil, <u>through and through</u>.
9 I like <u>springing surprises on</u> people.
10 His name's <u>on the tip of my tongue</u>.
11 If <u>worst comes to worst</u>, we can always …
12 Have you heard of the <u>Big Bang theory</u>?
13 She won <u>fair and square</u>.
14 There will be light <u>cloud cover</u> in the afternoon
15 You <u>drive a hard bargain</u>. Have you ever been a used car salesman?
16 In the old days, people worked from <u>dawn till dusk</u>.
17 Insurance and legal firms have got things going their way now – we're becoming a <u>blame 'n' claim</u> culture
18 She's <u>gone but not forgotten</u>.
19 <u>He likes playing pranks on</u> people. He's not very popular, as you can imagine.
20 What a mess! <u>Everything's all topsy-turvy</u>.
21 Visitors to the palace should <u>mind their manners</u>.
22 Their cellar is <u>a treasure trove</u> of photos from the 1800s.
23 I don't have a plan. I'm just going to <u>go with the flow</u>.
24 I don't want any talk about <u>shoulda, coulda, woulda</u>. Let's focus on the future.
25 Let's <u>hit him where it hurts</u>.
26 No re-negotiating. It's <u>a done deal</u>.
27 They're by far the best team. They've <u>made mincemeat of</u> the competition.
28 He's disgusting … <u>the lowest of the low</u>.
29 She's got <u>a screw loose</u>.
30 <u>There's more to her than meets the eye</u>.
31 Being an expert means really <u>knowing your onions</u> about something.
32 I <u>tried and tried, but couldn't</u> do it.
33 Let's not <u>play the blame game</u>, shall we?
34 Your <u>best bet</u> is to go by train.
35 Him, co-operate with anyone? With that <u>stubborn streak</u> of his? Not likely!

Idiom Explanations

Idiom Explanations for 4.1

1   **be _a nervous wreck_**   = be totally stressed out

At the same time as she was studying for her medical exams – which was stressing her out totally anyway – Mary was also going through a bitter divorce. And then her mother went into hospital with a serious heart problem. Then her landlord raised the rent, and she had no idea where she could find the extra money. That would be enough to turn anyone into a nervous wreck.

2   **_pin your hopes on_** something.   = put all your hopes onto one thing

She had pinned all her hopes on her parents loaning her some money. When they said they couldn't, she burst into tears.

3   **_hazard a guess (about something)_**   = make a rather uncertain guess

I have no idea how much he earns, but I'll hazard a guess that it's over a million.

4   I can't tell you **_off the top of my head_**   = I can't tell you immediately; I need time to think about it.

Off the top of my head, I think the population of London is about four million, but I don't really know for sure. If you want an exact answer, give me time to check on the internet.

5   She **_turned a blind eye to_** his cheating.   = She was aware of his cheating, but pretended she didn't notice.

She wanted to start again and learn from her experience. She decided she would be more assertive than before, when she had **_turned a blind eye_** to her husband's cheating.

6   It'll be **_plain sailing_** from now on.   = Everything will be problem free, without difficulty.

Some people say that the biggest problems with learning Chinese are the tones and the writing, but that if you learn those it's all **_plain sailing_** after that, because the grammar is fairly simple.

7   **_wear your heart on your sleeve_**   = show your romantic feelings openly, perhaps without being aware that you're doing so.

Poor man. He really does **_wear his heart on his sleeve_**. Everyone can see that he's in love with her. But she, for her part, hardly knows he exists.

8   Does that **_ring a bell with you_**?   = Do you have any memory of that?

I **think** it was Edinburgh we stayed in when we went to Scotland all those years ago. Does that **_ring a bell with you_**?

9   Her refusal **_knocked him off his perch_**.   = Her refusal caused him to suddenly lose confidence.

Full of confidence, he asked her to marry him. She said, "You!? What makes you think I'd marry you? I've never even liked you. And what, by the way, is your name?" That really **_knocked him off his perch_**!

10   **_look askance at_** sb   = look at sb in a sceptical way; or (figuratively) have doubts about the correctness of s'thing, sb, or sb's behaviour

Some finance officers might **_look askance at_** our high spending on 'entertainment' – but ours never complains or criticises.

Slips for the memory exercise

I'm a nervous wr.	I'm a n. wreck.
The farmers p. their hopes on rain.	The farmers pinned their h. on rain.
Go on, hazard a g.! How many?	Go on, h. a guess! How many?
I can't tell you off the t. of my head.	I can't tell you off the top of my h.
She t. a blind eye to his cheating.	She turned a bl. e. to his cheating.
He w. his heart on his sl.	He wears his h. on his sleeve
Does that r. a bell with you?	Does that ring a b. with you?
Her r. knocked him off his p.	Her refusal kn. him off his perch.
Whoopee! It's going to be p. sailing from now on.	Whoopee! It's going to be plain s. from now on.
Book lovers may l. askance at comic books.	Book lovers may look a. at comic books.

4.8 Example worksheets

Pre-intermediate

1 I forgot to bring a // pen. **Could I // borrow one of // yours**?

2 Have you ever // had **breakfast // in // bed**?

3 Yes, other people can come. // **The more // the // merrier**!

4 Russia is almost // **twice as // big // as** the United States.

5 I was going to tell you something but I've forgotten what it was. **Never // mind. It // wasn't // important**.

6 Excuse me. **Could you tell // me what // time // it is**?

7 I wanted to do my homework, **but I // couldn't // find // the time**.

8 I don't know this word. **Can you // tell me what // it // means**?

Intermediate

1 People who never brush their // teeth may have **// bad // breath**.

2 This train's been sitting here for a half an hour. **What on // earth could it be // waiting // for**?

3 It doesn't matter to me. I don't care at all. In // fact, **I couldn't // care // less**.

4 He told a joke, but no one // laughed. It // **fell // flat**.

5 She paid a lot for her new shoes because the shop assistant told her they would **// last a // life//time**.

6 Good news. Paul and Paula aren't angry with each other any more. They finally // kissed and **// made // up**.

7 Not so fast! You know what people say – **more // haste // less // speed**.

8 Sally and Steve have gone bankrupt. Now they'll have to build // a new life **// from // scratch**.

9 Excuse me. **Would you mind // taking a // photo of** my friend and // **me**?

Upper intermediate

1 Shy?! Her? Don't you believe it. She's // **as // bold as // brass**.

2 I don't think she insulted me unintentionally. I think she said what she said on purpose. I think her // remark was // **carefully // calculated.**

3 Go on, try. It's not hard. It's // **easy-//peasy.**

4 Oh! There's a scorpion on your collar! // **Don't // move a // muscle!**

5 Our neighbour's not very sociable. We don't see him much. He // **keeps // himself to // himself**.

6 You want to know about running a business? Talk to Barry. He **really // knows his // onions**.

7 What we've been doing isn't working. It's time we // **tried // Plan // B**.

8 You know, your sarcasm is something I // **could // do // without**.

9 You know Jack and Jill? They won the lottery and now they're // **sitting // pretty**.

10 When it comes to shirking // work, Lazy Bob's a // **past // master**.

4.9 Chunk Quiz

Upper intermediate

1 What word comes next after this? ***"It's a Catch-22 _____"***

2 If someone says, "Have a good weekend", what's a common, friendly reply?

3 If I ***bump into*** an old friend in the street, did we arrange to meet there?

4 Write down two idioms we've done that come from horse riding.

5 Write down four common phrases that contain colour words like 'red', 'blue', 'white', 'black'.

6 Write a true sentence containing the phrase ***if I can help it.***

7 Write a phrase we had this week which alliterates and which includes the word 'life'.

8 Are these pairs of dating and romance phrases in their normal order? Answer Yes or No for each pair:

   a) ***chat up, ask out***; b) ***hit it off, break up*** ; c) ***make up, have a row***

9 Say which kind of activity each of these phrases comes from.

   a) ***have an ace up your sleeve*** ; b) ***in the wake of***

10 I'm going to say some phrases which were in the newspaper article we read on (*the day you read it*) and some which weren't. Listen, and write down only the ones that ***were*** in the article:

   didn't show up on time, lost his cool, tossed and turned all night, did wonders for …

11 I'm going to say some verb idioms. For each one, write a short sentence saying who, in the short story we read on (*whenever*), did the action. For example, if I say, ***Hit it off***, you write, 'Barry and Jim hit it off'. OK? Here we go: ***Cracked under the pressure …***

12 I'm going to say some sentences, and if they're positive in meaning, write the sentence and a plus sign, and if they're negative, write the sentence and a minus sign. Ready? Here's the first one: ***I'm over the moon about it.*** Here's the second one: ***She's a very down-to-earth person …***

13 Write a true sentence using the verb 'dodge' in a well–known metaphor.

Sample text

Instructions: Insert the following phrases into the text below, fitting them as best you can into their natural places. Write each phrase in the correct place, as shown by the example: Once upon a time. Sometimes you will need to delete a word in the text, usually not. Sometimes you will need to change the punctuation or capitalisation of a letter.

---

but in vain / at first / in desperation / let alone / ~~Once upon a time~~ / Nothing worked

Once upon a time

⅄ There was a king and queen whose son never went anywhere. He never went out of the palace or to town. His parents thought that if they just waited he would decide to go somewhere; but several years passed and he still never went anywhere at all. Then they tried showing him pictures of the beautiful world outside and bought him some running shoes. They gave him maps and bus tickets. Finally they gave up and just ignored him. Now he is king; but he still doesn't go anywhere.

Hints

Pre-intermediate

Once upon a time, there was a king and queen whose daughter was always sad. Never did she smile, *le_ al___* laugh. Of course, her parents tried everything to bring a smile to her face. They paid clowns to come and *d_ tr___s* and comedians to come and *t___ jo__s*. Nothing! Trick after trick, joke after joke, the princess never smiled – *no_ ev__ once*, *no_ ev__ a little*. But cry! Oh, that's something she did ten times a day – if a cloud passed in front of the sun, if there was a bit of sand in her porridge, if she had a sad thought, if she hurt her finger when she picked a rose, if her kitten gave her a little scratch, if her soup was cold, and most especially if her favourite programme wasn't on TV because of a football game.

B_ the ti___ she was 17, her parents were completely *fe_ u_ wi__* her crying *desp___ the f_ct th__* her tears made their rose garden the most beautiful in the land. But, do you know, they had *never* taken the *p___r ___rl* to London? Not *in all her li__*, not since she had been born. Not once! Can you believe it!? Well, maybe it's not so surprising. Who would want to be in London with a girl who cried *a__ the ti___*? Well, anyway, one day, when the princess was 17, the king and queen *at __st decided to g__* to London and *ta___* their daughter *al___* with them. So they phoned a hotel and *ma___ a res_____* for the *bigg___ and be___* room in the whole hotel, for one whole month*!* The queen and king were very excited – so excited that they didn't notice that the princess looked even sadder *th__ us__l*.

So one Friday afternoon they all boarded a train *b___nd f___* Victoria Station in London. The king and queen (*b_ th_ w__*, they were not the king and queen of England) were really happy. They were really *l____ing ___ward t_* a whole month of visiting museums and *ar_ gal_____s* and seeing plays and films. The princess, however, had never looked sadder *i_ her __ole li__* than she did now. And after a few days her parents *____ldn't __lp b__t* notice how sad she looked. They began to worry about her again. But that night, the three of them were going to *ha__ di_____* in an expensive restaurant with another king and queen and their son, who was of course a prince.

The six of them met in the restaurant bar at about 8pm. This new king and queen were nothing special – just a very ordinary queen and a completely normal and typical king. The prince, however, was handsome. No, not just handsome but incredibly handsome. No, not just incredibly handsome, but gorgeous … a word not often used about men, you know!

continued …

And he was funny – and clever! So full of interesting stories! So polite! Tall. Considerate. And fit. (He skied, played polo, climbed Mount Everest every year at Christmas.) The princess's mother could _ot _eep her e___s __ff him. He was perfect!

The princess, though, looked at him for about one second **ou_ of the c___er of an e__**, and then began to cry because once again her soup was cold. How cruel the world seemed to her! But then her parents announced that it was her birthday. She had been so miserable recently that she had forgotten all about this. But when the prince **h___rd this _ews**, he stood up, bowed to the princess, and began to sing '**Ha___ Bi_____ T_ Y__'**. His voice was magical. He sang like a god. He was more than perfect! But just when he came to her name – Tracy … Princess Tracy – and had his mouth **wi__ o___**, a fly flew in. A big, black, ugly, fly. He closed his mouth. But everyone could hear the fly buzzing around inside. He coughed and out flew the fly along with the prince's false teeth which shot into his soup, splashing it **_ll ov__ the pl___**. The princess was the only one present who didn't get **cov____ ___th** soup (onion soup, if you want to know). Then the prince sneezed and fell backwards over his chair. As he was falling backwards, he **cr____ed in___** a waiter carrying a large tray of cakes and cups of hot coffee. The waiter fell onto a table **cov_____ __th** food and drink. It was a disaster! Was the princess sad now? Well, yes she was. Even this dinnertime disaster didn't make her laugh. Of course, her parents understood now that there was **n_ ho___ for** her. She would never laugh. So they did the only sensible thing. They moved to a new castle but never told her which one. The princess didn't mind though. She got together with the prince **aft__ _ll**. How? How do you think?

KEYS

KEYS

2.4
Intermediate
The Boy Who Cried Wolf (Aesop)

A shepherd boy had the job of watching over a flock of sheep near a village. In one week he summoned the villagers three times by crying out, "Wolf! Wolf!" When they <u>came running to help</u>, he laughed. "I was just <u>having fun,</u>" he said. And didn't they know it was boring being a shepherd <u>day in and day out</u>? <u>Not surprisingly</u>, the villagers cursed him <u>loud and long</u>. One day, though, a wolf *did* come. The shepherd boy yelled and yelled, "Wolf! Help! *Wolf!*" The villagers heard him, but no one came. <u>As a result</u>, the whole flock of sheep was lost – all killed by the wolf. And as punishment, the boy's parents <u>beat him black and blue</u>. The moral? People may not believe liars even when they <u>tell the truth</u>.

Intermediate–Upper intermediate

A Spanish couple have got the <u>green light</u> from a judge to evict their two sons, aged 19 and 20, <u>on the grounds that</u> living with them was <u>sheer hell</u>. The judge ruled that as the sons were adults, their parents were <u>no longer</u> <u>under any obligation</u> to <u>provide them with room and board</u>. The sons were ordered to <u>clear out of</u> <u>the family home</u> in a town in north east Spain.

2.5
Upper elementary

Tigers are big wild cats that live <u>here and there</u> in Asia, not Africa. They are very rare now. Most of them live in India, but there are a few in some other countries. There are even a few tigers in the part of Russia that is near North Korea. <u>Did you know that</u> they like to swim? They eat other animals. Sometimes they attack people. But most people think tigers are beautiful even if they are dangerous.

Pre-intermediate

<u>On her way home</u> after celebrating her birthday, a Belarus woman felt sleepy and lay down on what she thought was the ground. During the night a train ran right over her and she didn't wake up. <u>Believe it or not</u>, the place she picked to sleep was between the two rails of a train line. Doctors later said it was a good thing she didn't wake up and move while the train was passing over her. People who saw her lying on the train line in the morning thought she was dead and phoned the emergency services.

Intermediate
A true story

An Italian woman was in hospital to give birth. When the baby was born – and while the woman was still <u>laid up</u> in bed – the husband gave the little boy the names of his favourite horse and jockey. So the boy's first name was the name of the jockey and his middle name was the name of the horse – or maybe <u>the other way around</u>. You see, the husband was passionate about betting on horse races. The hospital officials accepted the strange name because the man told them that his wife had agreed to it. But she hadn't agreed! In fact, she didn't know about these crazy names at all! She was furious at her husband when she found out what he had done <u>behind her back</u>. When she came out of hospital, she went to court and asked for a change of name – from the strange, 'horsey' names to names that were more traditional. Perhaps later she also asked for a divorce!

Note 'laid up' means she was in bed in order to get well, not just to sleep.

Intermediate
The Goose that laid Golden Eggs (Aesop, adapted)

A long time ago, a farming couple who lived in the countryside and raised geese made an exciting discovery. One of their geese had begun to lay a golden egg every <u>single</u> Monday! As soon as the egg was laid, either the wife or the husband would take it to town, sell it, and begin spending the money <u>like it was water</u>. They began to spend so much money that soon they were <u>deep</u> in debt. They agreed that that one egg a week wasn't enough and so, one Tuesday, they killed it, hoping to get – who knows? – dozens or hundreds of eggs <u>all at once</u>! But inside the goose all they found was <u>blood and guts</u>. The moral? Being greedy for more can cost you what you already have.

2.7
Survivor

An amateur sailor endured 24 hours in the cold North Atlantic after being swept off his one-man sailing boat by towering waves. Searchers had given up hope for the man, who was barely alive when he was found on a beach in Norway. "If only I had stayed at home!" he later said.

2.10

play a <u>part</u>	look <u>at</u>	more <u>likely</u> to
the <u>toss</u> of a coin	in any <u>way</u>	account <u>for</u>
for a <u>start</u>	body–mass <u>index</u>	still a long way to <u>go</u>
load the <u>dice</u>	statistically <u>significant</u>	

2.13 Jumbled sentences

A plausible ordering is:
One day in a café …
He caught her eye and vice versa. (= She noticed him and thought he was cute, and vice versa.)
He decided to chat her up. (= talk to her in the hope of getting to know her better – a *lot* better)
They hit it off. (= They immediately have a very good relationship.)
During the next few weeks, they hung out a lot together. (= spent a lot of time together.)
They gradually fell in love.
One day he popped the question. (= asked, "Will you marry me?")
She said "Yes" and that meant they were engaged. (= <u>engaged to be married</u>)
But not long after that, they had a row and broke off their engagement.
But the next day, they both apologised and made up. (= stopped being angry with each other)
They set a date for the wedding.
The Big Day came and they tied the knot. (= got married)
How are they getting on now? Well, so far so good!

3.5 Upper intermediate device words

	List A		List B
1	a spade	1	an axe
2	a sieve	2	a screw
3	a rake	3	an oar
4	a belt	4	an hour-glass
5	a sledgehammer	5	a door mat
6	a comb	6	a wedge
7	barbed wire	7	a funnel

For advanced learners, add additional words – e.g. *a nut, a bolt, a spanner*UK*/wrench*US, *a hoe, a mop.*

3.5 Review Sheet

1	axe	8	wedge
2	spade	9	sledgehammer
3	hour-glass	10	belt
4	barbed wire	11	funnel
5	door mat	12	screw
6	rake	13	sieve
7	comb	14	oar

3.6 Handout 4, Jack and Jill

1	the stakes are low	L
2	raise the stakes	L
3	not their strong suit	F
4	an ace up their sleeve	L
5	Jack had all the aces	L
6	played his cards close to his chest	L
7	had the winning hand	L
8	threw in her hand	L
9	all the chips were down	L
10	the showdown	L
11	laid all their cards on the table	L
12	not on the cards	F
13	lay all my cards on the table	F
14	have one more ace up my sleeve	F
15	when the chips are down	L+F
16	an ace up her sleeve	L

3.6 Handout 5

1	close, chest	12	trumps, aces, cards
2	lay, table	13	joker, pack, wild
3	re-shuffle	14	chip
4	spades	15	stacked
5	cards	16	ante, stakes
6	winning hand	17	showdown
7	ace	18	tipped
8	trumps	19	play, cards, right
9	chips	20	poker
10	strong suit	21	chip
11	hand, folded hand		

3.6 Handout 6

1	cards, close, chest	11	threw
2	show	12	folded
3	cards out on the table	13	joker
4	in spades	14	chip
5	cards	15	stacked
6	aces	16	up
7	ace, sleeve	17	stakes
8	comes, trumps, end	18	showdown
9	chips	19	hole
10	strong suit	20	Blue chip

3.6 Idiom meanings

1   He plays his cards close to his chest.
   keeps his plans secret
2   It's time for everyone to
   say what they are thinking
   lay all their cards on the table.
3   The PM has announced a cabinet re-shuffle.
   a re-organisation
4   She didn't just win – she won in spades!
   emphatically, clearly, by a wide margin
5   It's not on the cards[UK]/in the cards[US].
   not possible
6   We've got the winning hand.
   most or all of the advantages
7   I've got an ace in the hole/up my sleeve.
   a secret advantage
8   She always turns up trumps in the end.
   does a great job when it really matters
9   You can always rely on her
   in a deciding, end-game, situation
   when the chips are down.
10 Mathematics is not my strong suit.

my best talent
11 He threw in his hand. = He folded (his hand).
   gave up, quit
12 We're holding all the trumps / aces / high cards.
   all the advantages
13 He's the joker in the pack/the wild card.
   the unpredictable one
14 Do you mind if I chip in?
   contribute (i.e. pay part of a bill, or add s'thing into a conversation)
15 The cards are stacked against us.
   Things are against us.
16 It's time to up the ante.
   increase the investment and
   = It's time to raise the stakes.
   so increase the risk.
17 The PM had a showdown with his chancellor
   a decisive confrontation
   over the issue of interest rates.
18 She tipped her hand.
   gave a hint about her intentions (accidentally or on purpose)
19 If you play your cards right, you might succeed.
   make good use of your resources & opportunities
20 Try to keep a poker face during the negotiation.
   not show your thoughts or feelings
21 Being a very conservative investor,
   highly valued
   I only invest in blue chip companies.

3.7 Jigsaw text questions

Text 1
a)   The Royal Navy and the Merchant Navy
b)   No, not any more. The American and Russian navies were much bigger by the 1970s.
c)   To show the importance of seafaring in British culture.
d)   It was also very big.
e)   Yes, ferries are still quite important even though they are no longer the only way to travel to and from Britain.
f)   No, although it is true that men and boys living near the sea were relatively likely to o to sea.
g)   Seafaring meant that quite a few families lacked a husband and father for much of the time.

Text 2
a)   North Africa (especially the part that is now Morocco, Algeria and Tunisia).
b)   They used them as slaves (although they also sometimes held them for ransom – this was a big 'industry' among the Moors for about a thousand years!)
c)   Spanish gold.
d)   The big European naval powers such as Spain, France, the Netherlands and England were busy fighting other Europeans, often in wars of religion. Also, England had a weak and divided government for much of this time.
e)   Most were, but not all.
f)   Pirates. Also sometimes called 'buccaneers'.

Text 3
a)   To give examples of sea-related employment besides the jobs of actually being a sailor.
b)   There are hundreds of them. They are like parking places for yachts and boats – both motor boats and sailing boats. Many marinas are linking with yacht clubs and sailing clubs.
c)   To give another example that sailing is not at all dead as a British pastime.

) On the contrary, lots do.
) The National Maritime (i.e. seafaring) Museum.
To give another example of the importance of seafaring in British life.
) We are going to learn some!

3.7 Explanations of idiom sentences

Learn the ropes = learn the basics of a new job.
Old-time sailing ships had dozens of ropes, each with its own name and function. The sailors who worked on deck had to know the name and function of each rope. So each new sailor had to 'learn the ropes' in order to do his job.
E.g. In every new job it takes a while to <u>learn the ropes</u>.
Take the helm / be at the helm = become / be the director.
The 'helm' is the steering wheel, near or at the back of a sailing ship. The person who is 'at the helm' controls the direction of the ship.
E.g. When the president died, the vice-president <u>took the helm</u>.
(Do s'thing) **under your own steam** = do it without help.
An old nautical phrase meaning that the ship or boat is moving is 'under way'. So when steamships were invented, a natural way to speak of them moving was 'under steam'. If a steamship broke down and had to be pulled by another ship, it was not going 'under its own steam'. Therefore, to be under your own steam means to do something without help.
E.g. She needed lots of help while she was learning the ropes, but now she's running <u>under her own steam</u>.
To give sb a wide berth = avoid, not go near.
A 'berth' is the space for one ship when it is tied up to the dockside in port. In the old days, if a ship was believed to be carrying disease, the operators of the
port would give it a 'wide berth' so that other ships did not have to be
too near it. E.g. I don't trust that guy. I'm going to <u>give him a wide berth</u>.
To keel over = fall over suddenly and unexpectedly, esp. because of illness.
The keel is the long, strong, heavy, narrow bottom part of a ship. The keel runs from the front of a ship to the back like a backbone. If a ship 'keels over', then the boat has rolled so much that the keel shows above the water.
E.g. She turned white and then <u>just keeled over</u>, hitting her head as she fell.
H**ave (enough/a little…) leeway** = (enough) freedom from restrictions.
Imagine a ship sailing near the shore. If the wind is blowing towards the land from the sea, the wind could push the ship onto the shore, which would be disastrous for the ship. In such a case, the 'leeway' is the distance between the ship and the shore. The stronger the wind, the more leeway the ship needs. In everyday life, having 'leeway' means having enough freedom of movement or, metaphorically, sufficient freedom to do what you want to do.
E.g. I wish the boss would <u>give me</u> more <u>leeway</u>. I'm under such tight control that I can't take advantage of opportunities that come up quickly.
Everything's shipshape. = neat and tidy, in good order.
On a ship there may be little space for many people. Neatness and order are extremely important.
E.g. **Everything's shipshape** and ready for inspection.
To try a different tack = try a new way of doing s'thing.
If a sailing ship is trying to go in the direction the wind is blowing from, it cannot move in a straight line. Instead, it must zig-zag left and right. Each change of direction is 'a tack'.

E.g. She tried to learn French by reading novels but it didn't work very well, so she <u>tried a different tack</u> – she hired a private teacher.

9 **Be on an even keel** = be/feel emotionally balanced.
In a stormy sea, the keel of a ship is not even (= level); in a calm sea it is.
E.g. She hasn't been <u>on an even keel</u> since she lost her job.

10 It was all **plain sailing**. = problem-free.
Plain sail was the normal set of sails, used when the weather was good.

11 Don't **rock the boat** = Don't cause trouble in an organisation by criticising or trying to change the way things are traditionally done. E.g. If you're in the armed forces, you can get in trouble by trying to <u>rock the boat</u>.

12 **In the wake of** an important event or disaster = at the time just after (an important event or disaster) and probably caused by it. The 'wake' is the trail of disturbed water that follows a moving boat or ship.
E.g. There were riots <u>in the wake of</u> the king's assassination.

3.8 Horse Idioms and Sayings

1 *keeps a tight rein on*
a) keeps firm control over
2 *unbridled passion*
b) uncontrolled passion
3 *spur … on*
b) cause … to work harder and go faster
4 *at the end of my tether*
b) at the limit of my mental strength and patience
5 *Give free rein to*
a) Release, set free
6 *a one horse race*.
b) not a close contest at all
7 *be a spur to*
a) encourage
8 *Stop horsing around*
b) Stop playing and being foolish
9 *Wild horses couldn't keep me away*.
a) Nothing could stop me from coming
10 *put the cart before the horse*.
a) Don't do things in the wrong order.
11 *You can lead a horse to water but you can't make it drink*.
b) You can give people advice but you can't usually make them follow it.
12 *a one horse town*.
b) a small, quiet town where little ever happens
13 *Saddled with debt*
a) carrying a heavy load of debt.
14 *galloping inflation*
b) a very *rapid* increase in prices
15 disagreement *reared its ugly head*.
b) People began to disagree.

3.9 Full key to Little Red Riding Hood

put your foot in it – F
off the top of her head – L
off the top of my head – F
gave him the cold shoulder – F
got cold feet – F
head over heels – L
put a foot wrong – L
played it by ear – F (but not metaphorical. Instead this chunk is 'metonymic' ie. 'ear' stands for Little Red Riding Hood's whole musical ability, of which one of her ears was only a part.)
play it by ear – F

couldn't carry a tune in a basket – F
got cold feet – L
offhand – F
from head to toe – L
put his foot in his mouth – L
by heart – F
wear your heart on your sleeve – L, perhaps also F
from head to toe – F
out of hand – F
on tiptoe - L

3.10 Exercise Sheet

1 flex their muscles
2 lower his guard
3 stick his neck out
4 take it on the chin
5 not pull their punches
6 throw in the towel
7 out for the count
8 the gloves are off
9 'He's on the ropes now'
   (because although a boxer in a tight corner is in a bad position, a boxer who has been forced against the ropes is in a worse one)

3.11 What *it* originally stood for:

a 9
b 10
c 1
d 11

e 12
f 8
g 7
h 2

i 5
j 6
k 15
l 4

m 14
n 13
o 3

3.13:2

The chunks shown in *italic* are those that are figurative **and** relate to emotion.
Figurative expressions of anger that are not common chunks are underlined.
There are of course other types of chunk in the text – such as **nearest and dearest –** but these do not qualify as answers to this exercise, so are not shown in italic.

It has become a widely accepted idea in western culture that instead of **bottling up our emotions** we should air them now and then. For example, if we're frustrated, **ventilating our feelings**, or **blowing off steam**, may help us to avoid any sudden **explosion of emotion**. But this can generate a serious problem. As it happens, **releasing**, or **ventilating, anger** is a particularly bad way to **cool down**. An **outburst of rage** typically **pumps us up**, making us feel **more** angry, not less. And if we **reach boiling point** and **blow up at someone** who has provoked our anger*, our rage reaches a yet higher peak, and our angry mood is prolonged. Also, we may well **erupt in rage** even at innocent bystanders – and, worse, our nearest and dearest – and continue to fume much longer after our **outburst** than if we had not **unleashed our rage**.
A far more effective way of managing anger is to take advantage of our human ability to 'step back' mentally, and observe our own feelings and behaviour. This naturally results in us **simmering down**, without any further effort on our part. It also gives us the opportunity to look at the issue from the other person's viewpoint, so that we can constructively seek a solution with them.
Based on Goleman (2006) and S. N. Goenka (Vipassana, December 2007)
* If you know Latin well, *provoke anger* may also be metaphorical since 'provoke' comes from the Latin for 'call forth' (i.e. provocare).

3.14 Worksheet

Commit: **adultery, arson, a burglary, a crime, a murder, a robbery, an assault, an offence, an atrocity, suicide**
Conduct: **a ceremony, a study, a survey, , an experiment, an inquiry, an inspection, an interview, an investigation, research**
Conduct (also carry out): **an inspection, research**
Perform: **a ceremony, a dance, a miracle, a play, a solo, a song**
Cause: **damage, destruction, devastation, havoc.**

3.15

The verb + -ing sentences are 3, 4, 6, 9, 13, 15.
Explanation:
1 & 2   in time order; **be healthy** is a goal.
3   not in time order; meeting her was not necessarily a goal
4   not in time order; contributing was the opposite of a goal
5   in time order; phoning was similar to a goal
6   not in time order; smoking was not the goal
7 & 8   in time order
9   not in time order; leaving is not the goal of regretting
10–12   in time order; the second verb is a kind of goal
13   leaving is not yet a goal.
14   in time order; coming was the goal of whoever did the forcin
15   not in time order.

3.16

Pre-intermediate
1   Keep ~~approaching~~! / **c**oming
2   **d**ropped / ~~fell~~ dead
3   The ~~blackest~~ / **d**arkest hour
4   **F**orbidden / ~~taboo~~ fruit
5   a ~~new~~ / **f**resh ~~person~~ / **f**ace
6   the ~~boss~~ / **h**ead of the house
7   a ~~strange~~ / **f**unny feeling
8   as good as ~~silver~~ / **g**old
9   watch the ~~plants~~ / **g**rass grow
10   to make ~~things~~ / **m**atters worse
11   as **p**retty / ~~lovely~~ as a picture
12   When the cat's away the mice will ~~have a good time~~ / pl**a**y
13   from hero to ~~nothing~~ / **z**ero
14   The ~~larger~~ / **b**igg**e**r the better
15   in ~~fine~~ / gr**e**at shape
16   a fight to the **f**inish / ~~end~~
17   one big, ~~glad~~ / h**a**ppy family
18   a deep ~~black~~ / **d**ark secret
19   ~~money~~ / **c**ash in hand
20   to ~~leave~~ / **h**ead for home

Intermediate
1   too big for his ~~shoes~~ / **b**oots
2   ~~in prison~~ / behind **b**ars
3   in slow ~~movement~~ / m**o**tion
4   can't **b**ear / ~~carry~~ this heavy burden
5   well colour **c**o-ordinated / ~~matched~~
6   to be ~~nasty~~ / **c**ruel to be kind
7   too **c**lose / ~~near~~ for comfort
8   God's ~~present~~ / **g**ift (to women)
9   good ~~act~~ / **d**eed for the day
10   Look before ~~you jump~~ / **l**eap
11   so deadly **d**ull / ~~boring~~
12   foreign aff**a**irs / ~~relations~~
13   **w**ell / ~~very~~ aware
14   facts and **f**igures / ~~numbers~~
15   on its last ~~feet~~ / **l**egs
16   fatal ~~imperfection~~ / **f**law
17   head over ~~feet~~ / **h**eels in love
18   Love her or ~~hate~~ / **l**oathe her
19   in slow ~~movement~~ / m**o**tion
20   cares and **c**oncerns / ~~worries~~

21 could **g**et / ~~rise~~ off the ground
22 such ~~intense~~ / **h**igh hopes
23 the ~~starring~~ / **l**eading **l**ady / ~~actress~~
24 disaster may ~~happen~~ / **s**trike
25 looks could **k**ill / ~~murder~~
26 a no go ~~area~~ / **z**one
27 to make ~~things~~ / matters worse
28 **m**ixed / ~~confused~~ emotions
29 **n**ext / ~~close~~ to nothing
30 born with a ~~golden~~ / **s**ilver spoon in his mouth
31 start from ~~zero~~ / **s**cratch
32 signs of a **s**truggle / ~~fight~~
33 I hope you're ~~glad~~ / **h**appy
34 fair and ~~honest~~ / sq**uare**
35 never li**f**ted / ~~raised~~ a finger
36 **shu**t / ~~close~~ up shop
37 ~~maintain~~ / k**ee**p the peace

Upper intermediate
1 Beauty is in the eye of the **b**eholder / ~~viewer~~ *
2 worldly **w**ealth / ~~assets~~
3 ~~over~~ / a**b**ove and beyond
4 in word and dee**d** / ~~action~~
5 has ~~changed~~ / **t**aken a **tur**n for the worse
6 beyond the **b**ounds / ~~limits~~
7 a whole ~~crowd~~ / **ho**st
8 the courage of their ~~beliefs~~ / **c**onvictions
9 broken the ~~legs~~ / **b**ack of this problem
10 ~~disappearing~~ / **v**anishing act
11 bet your ~~shoes~~ / **b**oots
12 **p**et / ~~favourite~~ project
13 a ~~general~~ / **b**lanket ban
14 loophole / ~~gap~~ in the law
15 one bit / **cr**um**b** of comfort
16 code of **c**onduct / ~~rules of behaviour~~
17 to ~~win against~~ / **g**ain ground on the opposition
18 on its last ~~feet~~ / **l**egs
19 Low ~~altitude~~ / **l**ying land
20 made her life a ~~tragedy~~ / **m**isery
21 a rather ~~general~~ / **s**weeping statement
22 knows his ~~carrots~~ / o**n**ions
23 Not all is gold that ~~shines~~ / **g**listens
24 the main ~~focus~~ / bo**n**e of contention
25 the paper it's ~~written~~ / **p**rinted on
26 **p**urchasing / ~~buying~~ power
27 doesn't ~~sound~~ / **r**ing true
28 pretty ~~shocking~~ / gr**i**m reading
29 a serious ~~reversal~~ / **s**etback
30 ~~literature~~ / **p**oetry in motion
31 a real test of **st**amina / ~~endurance~~
32 a twist in the ~~ending~~ / tail
33 worldly **w**ealth / ~~riches~~
34 Naming and ~~disgracing~~ / sh**aming**
35 this late ~~day~~ / d**ate**
36 the **w**orthy / ~~deserving~~ winner
37 well ~~inside~~ / **w**ithin budget
38 It's a top **notch** / ~~quality~~ product **
39 She was ~~pulling out~~ / **tear**ing her hair in desperation
40 call a ~~stop~~ / ha**l**t
41 goes to sh**ow** / ~~prove~~
42 last ~~breath~~ / **g**asp attempt
* Although 'viewer' is assonant with 'beauty', it seems that
   alliteration trumps assonance.
** Short words trump long ones.

Advanced
1 more **b**ang for your buck / ~~results for your dollar~~
2 **st**age-struck / ~~attracted by the theatre~~
3 brains and ~~muscles~~ / **br**aw**n**
4 former ~~condition~~ / gl**o**ry
5 begging **b**owl / ~~plate~~
6 that's the way the **c**ookie / ~~biscuit~~ crumbles
7 were you born in a ~~stable~~ / **b**arn ?
8 fighting was ~~close up~~ / at close **q**uarters
9 Every **d**og / ~~cat~~ has its day
10 look farther ~~away~~ / a**f**ield
11 little miss bossy **b**oots / ~~shoes~~
12 Don't ~~cause me any trouble~~ / **g**ive me any **g**rief
13 the head **h**oncho / ~~person~~
14 the **l**ie / ~~contours~~ of the land
15 lost its ~~shine~~ / **l**ustre
16 much **m**aligned / ~~criticised~~
17 It's of **p**aramount / ~~great~~ importance
18 beyond the **b**ounds / ~~limits~~
19 the ~~rule~~ / n**ame** of the game is publish or ~~die~~ / p**er**ish
20 was **p**illoried / ~~sharply criticised~~ in the press
21 Rumours are ~~everywhere~~ / **r**ife
22 living in rather **s**traitened / ~~impoverished~~ circumstances
23 A certain **s**omebody / ~~you-know-who~~
24 a ~~little~~ / **s**neaking suspicion
25 that ~~attack~~ / a**ss**ault the senses
26 the best ~~intentions~~ / **w**ill in the world
27 shopping ~~binges~~ / **s**prees
28 say boo to a ~~duck~~ / g**oo**se
29 media ~~tycoon~~ / moghul

3.17
Alliteration + Assonance (but in unstressed syllables) **+ Consonance**
10 **Forgive** and **forget**.

Alliteration + Assonance (but in unstressed syllables) **+ Word repetition**
30 **The bigger the better**.

Alliteration + Assonance
2 They **made** a **mis**take.
11 You look as **pretty** as a **pict**ure.
17 **Keep** it **clean**.

Alliteration + Consonance
5 The **m**ore the **m**errier.
25 There's **b**ad **b**lood between them.

Alliteration
1 He has a **b**eer **b**elly.
6 They **t**ook a **t**rip around the world.
9 Let's not wait. It's **n**ow or **n**ever.
14 What a **m**ess you've **m**ade!
18 **T**ell the **t**ruth.
33 Let's give our first speaker a **w**arm **w**elcome!
35 He likes being a **h**ouse **h**usband.

Assonance
7 Airport book shops mainly have **best-sell**ers.
8 She just got back from a w**orld** t**our** [US].
13 Have you got good or bad **eyesight**?
19 Did you **find** the **time** to phone her?
20 Is that the **right size** for you?
21 Take a **good look**.
23 **How** a**bout** going to the beach?
24 Do I hear **wed**ding **bell**s?
28 Let's do it right now. The **time** is **right**.
31 I **see** what you **mean**.
32 She visits her family on a **dail**y **bas**is.

Consonance

3 The s**torm** did a lot of **dam**age.

22 Do it **as fast as you can.**

34 Yes, that's an im**portant point.** Thank you for mentioning it.

Rhyme

4 Let's **bake** a **cake.**

Word repetition

12 It rained all day, **on and on.**

16 That happens **from time to time.**

26 We've never spoken **face to face.**

29 Things are getting better, **little by little.**

Nothing

15 It's **up to you.** (= the decision is yours)

27 We don't give credit. It's **pay as you go.**

4.10 Proposed key

Once upon a time there was a king and queen whose son never went anywhere. He never went out of the palace **let alone** or to town. **At first**, his parents thought that if they just waited, he would decide to go somewhere; but several years passed and still he never went anywhere at all. Then they tried showing him pictures of the beautiful world outside and bought him some running shoes, **but in vain. In desperation,** they gave him maps and bus tickets. **Nothing worked** so finally they gave up and just ignored him. Now he is king; but he still doesn't go anywhere.

4.11 Gapped text

let alone	decided to go to	not keep her eyes off
do tricks	take … along	out of the corner of an eye
tell jokes	made a reservation	heard this news
not even	biggest and best	'Happy Birthday To You'
not even	than usual	wide open
by the time	bound for	all over the place
fed up with	by the way	covered with
despite the fact that	looking forward to	crashed into
poor girl	art galleries	covered with
in all her life	in her whole life	no hope for
all the time	couldn't help but	after all
at last	have dinner	

4.12 Ideas:

- split chunks in half, jumble the halves and then ask students to re-assemble the chunks

- split sentences in half such that there is a chunk in one half or the other, e.g. 'On your first day at work // someone usually *shows you the ropes*'. The halves of sentences are jumbled up. Students have to re-assemble them

- jumble up the words of individual chunks (ones of more than three words) and students have to put the words back in order again (e.g. about the beat bush > ***beat about the bush***)

- anagramize (some of) the words in chunks; students then have to unjumble the letters (e.g. tbea about the shub)

- ask students to translate chunks

- ask students to match chunks to meanings (which you have helpfully provided on the test sheet)

- give students paraphrases or translations and ask them to write the corresponding chunk. To help, you can supply prompts/hints such as, e.g. b____ ab___ the ____, or … if you are artistic, a sketch.

- ask students to use each target chunk in a sentence which indicates the meaning of the chunk.

- divide chunks into sets according to origin (e.g. seafaring) or type of sound pattern (e.g., alliteration) or over-arching meaning or theme (e.g. anger/irritation) or positivity of connotation (e.g. a slimy character, a silky voice)

- order chunks chronologically, e.g.

> fall asleep, get dressed, go to bed, ~~get up~~, go to work, go home, get ready for work

1. get up   2.   3.   4.   5.   6.   7.

(Key: 1. get up 2. get dressed 3. get ready for work 4. go to work   5. go home 6. go to bed 7. fall asleep)

- read out a story or a series of sentences, and students write down – and properly spell! – chunks which you highlight, e.g. by saying, "When I click my fingers and then say a phrase and then click my fingers at the end of it, write down the phrase between the clicks."

- give students texts in which some (highlighted) chunks are used figuratively, some are used literally, and some are used ambiguously. Students say how each of the highlighted chunks has been used.

- as a variation of the translation task, read out a text or a series of sentences in English except that some times you use the mother tongue instead of an English chunk. At each of those points, students should write down an appropriate English chunk.

- compose True/False questions that have chunks in them such that students need to understand the chunks in order to be able to answer the questions rather than just guess.

- play a song, read out a text, show a video (etc.) Students have jumbled lists of chunks which are in the song/text or portrayed in the video. Students have to put the chunks in order according to what they hear or see.

- do movements: students write a chunk describing the movement. E.g. you say, "OK, number 1," and then conspicuously pick up a pencil. Students write 'pick up'.

- compose texts into which a stipulated set of chunks could be inserted. Students insert them appropriately.

- find a text with chunks in it, and swap certain chunks around so that none is in its original location. Then underline the chunks that have been swapped around. Students have to put them back in their original locations.

- compose Odd One Out quiz items, e.g: ***fall for***, ***hit it off***, ***brush off***

- give students lists of chunks in stories or songs they have met very recently. Students say which story/song the chunk was in (e.g. 'Hansel and Gretel'). If it's in a story, they get bonus points for correctly stating which character uttered the chunk, who they said it to, and when.

GLOSSARY

- A **chunk of language** is a common partnership between two or more words. Some of the many alternate terms for *chunk* are: *multi-word vocabulary, lexical phrase,* and *formulaic sequence.* Chunks include idioms, proverbs, common collocations (e.g., *heavy rain*) and phrasal verbs. It is assumed that a chunk is stored in memory as if it were a single word.

- **Elaborative processing** (also called 'deep' or 'rich' processing) of a chunk occurs when a learner thinks about the form and/or meaning of the chunk in ways that add detail to her/his knowledge of the chunk. Elaborative processing tends to result in the second kind of entrenchment described just below.

- **Entrenchment** of a chunk happens when memory traces in the brain become stronger because (1) **existing** connections between particular neurons become stronger and more active, and/or (2) a memory trace becomes easier to find through **new** connections being made from it to other memory traces.

- **(Linguistic) motivation** is what partly explains why a particular combination of words has become a/the accepted way of saying something. For instance, why do we say _beer_ _belly_ instead of *ale belly, food belly* or *beer tummy*? Part of the answer is the catchy b–b repetition which has 'motivated' (i.e. influenced) native speakers of English to accept this phrase as a natural-sounding way of referring to a particular kind of protruding belly. Chunks which are motivated are relatively easy to remember.

- A **mnemonic** is a technique or procedure a learner may use to remember vocabulary through use of memory prompts.

- **Rehearsal** is repeated mental processing of the form – and, ideally, also the meaning – of a chunk. Rehearsal of a foreign language chunk can be something as simple as writing the chunk down, turning the paper over, waiting ten seconds and trying to remember what you wrote. Successful rehearsal makes the chunk easier to remember, resulting in the first kind of entrenchment described above. The activities in Chapters 2 and 4 focus mainly on rehearsal.

- **Usage restrictions** are limitations on the use of a word or chunk – limitations which cannot easily be guessed from knowing its dictionary meaning and part of speech (or syntactic role). For example, knowing that *run aground* as defined in a dictionary means 'come to an unexpected stop, fail' will allow a learner to use this chunk wrongly, as in 'His car ran aground halfway through the race'. However, learners who know that *run aground* has to do with a ship becoming stuck in water that is not deep enough for it have a much better chance of remembering that this chunk is usually used for things that have something in common with ships – and this can be either literally or metaphorically, e.g. both ships and projects can be launched and both are said to run aground.

- A **word string** (cf a 'string of pearls') is a natural sequence of words which may or may not form a chunk.

BIBLIOGRAPHY

References

Arnold, J. Puchta, H. & M. Rinvolucri 2007. *Imagine That! Mental Imagery in the EFL Classroom.* Helbling Languages.

Collins Cobuild Dictionary of Idioms. 2002, 2nd ed. Collins.

Davis, P. & M. Rinvolucri. 1988. *Dictation: New Methods, New Possibilities.* Cambridge University Press.

Goleman, D. 2006. *Emotional Intelligence.* Bantam Dell.

The Macmillan English Dictionary for Advanced Learners, 2nd ed. 2007. Macmillan Education.

Oxford Collocations Dictionary for Students of English. 2002. Diana Lea, ed. Oxford University Press.

Oxford Phrasal Verbs Dictionary for Learners of English. 2006. Oxford University Press.

Further reading
Background to the approach
used in this book

Boers, F. 2000. Metaphor awareness and vocabulary retention. *Applied Linguistics*, 21: 553–571.

Boers, F., J. Eyckmans & H. Stengers. 2006. 'Motivating multiword units: Rationale, mnemonic benefits, and cognitive style variables.' In: S.H. Foster-Cohen, M.M. Krajnovic & J.M. Djigunovic eds., *EUROSLA Yearbook*, 6: 169–190, Amsterdam/ Philadelphia: John Benjamins.

Boers, F., J. Eyckmans & H. Stengers. 2007. Presenting figurative idioms with a touch of etymology: More than mere mnemonics? *Language Teaching Research*, 11/1: 43–62.

Boers, F. and S. Lindstromberg (eds.). 2008. *Cognitive Linguistic Approaches to Teaching Vocabulary and Phraseology.* Berlin / New York: Mouton de Gruyter.

Boers, F. and S. Lindstromberg. Forthcoming. *Optimizing a Lexical Approach to Instructed Second Language Acquisition.* Basingstoke: Palgrave Macmillan.

Lindstromberg, S. & F. Boers. 2008a. The mnemonic effect of noticing alliteration in lexical chunks. *Applied Linguistics*, 29/2: 200-22.

Lindstromberg, S. & F. Boers. 2008b. Phonemic repetition and the learning of lexical chunks: The mnemonic power of assonance. *System,* 36/3: 423-36.

Learning foreign
language vocabulary

Laufer, B. 1997. 'What's in a word that makes it hard or easy: some interlexical factors that affect the learning of words.' In N. Schmitt and M. McCarthy (eds.), *Vocabulary: Description, Acquisition,* Pedagogy, pp. 140–55. Cambridge University Press.

Laufer, B. 2005. 'Focus on Form in second language vocabulary acquisition.' In *EUROSLA Yearbook 5*, Susan Foster-Cohen (ed.), 223–250. John Benjamins.

Nation, I.S.P. 2001. *Learning Vocabulary in Another Language.* Cambridge: Cambridge University Press.

Nation, I.S.P. & P. Gu. 2007. *Focus on Vocabulary.* Macquarie University, Sydney: NCELTR Publications.

Schmitt, N. 1997. Vocabulary learning strategies. In *Vocabulary: Description, Acquisition and Pedagogy,* N. Schmitt, and M. McCarthy eds., pp. 199–236. Cambridge University Press.

Sökmen, A. J. 1997. 'Current trends in teaching second language vocabulary.' In *Vocabulary: Description, Acquisition and Pedagogy*, N. Schmitt and M. McCarthy, eds., pp. 237–257. Cambridge University Press.

Thompson, I. 1987. 'Memory in language learning.' In *Learner Strategies in Language Learning*, A. Wenden and J. Rubin eds., pp. 43–56. Prentice-Hall.

TEACHER'S QUICK - REFERENCE GUIDE

This guide will help you select an activity suitable for your class based on the time you have available and the learning level(s) of your students.

To use it, look down the left-hand column till you come to a time that's suitable for you, and then across to see the name of the activity in a cell spread across the range of levels it's suited to. Then across again to find the activity number.

Or if you prefer to start with the level of your students, go downwards till you find an activity name, and on that same row you will find the time required and the activity number.

Please note, however, that the time guide is only very basic; it does not take account of any extension. It merely allows you to see, when you're thinking of running an activity for the first time, how long the activity is likely to take. When you look at the details of the activity, you may find that the time is more flexible than appears in this guide.

Lesson time (mins)	Beginner	Elementary	Upper elementary	Pre-intermediate	Intermediate	Upper intermediate	Advanced	Activity no
Chapter 2 Initial steps								
Variable				Phrasal verbs via paired associates				2.12
5–10		Priming with Chinese whispers						2.2
5–10	Writing then reconstructing							2.6
10–15				Reading out loud with pauses				2.1
10–30				Teach your phrase				2.11
15–30			What are those initials for?					2.4
15–30			Remember my change					2.5
20–40			Dicto-composition: from chunks to text and back					2.8
20–40			Questionnaires with multiple choice answers					2.9
30–40				Situational clichés				2.14
45–60					Filling in a story skeleton			2.7
50–60					Between -listening gap fills			2.10
10 + 5–10	Memorising short dialogues							2.3
45 + 45				Putting chunks into chronological order: romantic relationships				2.13

Lesson time (mins)	Beginner	Elemen-tary	Upper elementary	Pre-intermediate	Intermediate	Upper intermediate	Advanced	Activity no
Chapter 3 Helping students remember chunks								
3–30				Figurative manner-of-action expressions				3.3
20–30					Seeing the deep logic of word partnerships			3.14
20–40				Sorting by sound				3.17
30–40						Talking about an emotion		3.13
30–45						Boxing idioms		3.10
30–45					Stop to smoke? Stop smoking?			3.15
30+					Sorting figurative idioms by source domain			3.12
40				Things that smell				3.1
40					Things that make sounds			3.2
40–50						Device idioms		3.5
40–60					What does *it* mean here?			3.11
45–60					Horse idioms			3.8
45–60					Body idioms			3.9
45–70				Noticing patterns of sound repetition				3.16
50					Weather phrases			3.4
45 + 45 + 45						Idioms from card-playing		3.6
45 + 45 + 45						Idioms from seafaring		3.7

Lesson time (mins)	Beginner	Elemen-tary	Upper elementary	Pre-intermediate	Intermediate	Upper intermediate	Advanced	Activity no
Chapter 4 Reviewing								
< 5					Student quizmasters			4.12
5–10	Review posters option 1							4.6
5–15				Guess my chunk				4.7
5–20						Memory slips with hints		4.1
5–20				What comes next?				4.5
10				Test me easy, test me hard				4.8
10		Blanks with big fat hints						4.11
10–15	Review posters option 2							4.6
10–30	Spoken team quizzes							4.9
10+		Embedding chunks in a text						4.10
15–20					Literal? Figurative? Either? Both?			4.2
15–25				Circulating review sheets				4.3
20–25				Using chunks in mini-stories				4.4

NOTES